Waukegan
Fire Department

Established 1849

Turner®
Publishing Company
Nashville, Tennessee • Paducah, Kentucky

TURNER PUBLISHING COMPANY

200 4th Avenue North • Suite 950
Nashville, Tennessee 37219
(615) 255-2665
www.turnerpublishing.com

Copyright 2009: Waukegan Fire Department
Publishing Rights: Turner Publishing Company

ISBN: 978-1-59652-163-6
Library of Congress Control Number: 2007931884

Printed in the United States of America
0 9 8 7 6 5 4 3 2 1

Contents

Mayor's Letter

City of

Waukegan

100 N. Martin Luther King Jr. Avenue
Waukegan, Illinois 60085
www.waukeganweb.net
✆ (847) 599-2500

Richard H. Hyde, Mayor
Wayne Motley, City Clerk
Patrick M. Dutcher, Treasurer

Greetings to our Members and Friends of the Waukegan Fire Department,

On behalf of the City of Waukegan, we extend our best wishes to all members of the Waukegan Fire Department. Over the years, our firefighters have served a vital role to protect our city from many different types of emergencies including fires, rescue situations, and emergency medical service calls.

We also express our heartfelt appreciation to all retired members of the Waukegan Fire Department who have served our city with dedication and distinction. Public safety is the foundation of any successful community and I am proud to say that the residents of Waukegan have an outstanding Fire Department to protect them.

On behalf of the City Council, we offer our congratulations to the Officers, Firefighters, and civilian members of the Waukegan Fire Department on this inaugural history book.

Thank you for your service to our community!

Sincerely,

Richard H. Hyde
Mayor
City of Waukegan

Mayor and Aldermen

Richard H. Hyde
Mayor

Wayne Motley
City Clerk

Patrick M. Dutcher
Treasurer

Sam Cunningham
1st Ward

John Balen
2nd Ward

Greg Mosio
3rd Ward

Tony Figueroa
4th Ward

Edith Newsome
5th Ward

Lawrence TenPas
6th Ward

Patrick Needham
7th Ward

Rick Larsen
8th Ward

Rafael Rivera
9th Ward

Chief's Letter

Message from the Fire Chief

EST. 1849

01 February 2008

Dear Members, Retirees, and Friends,

It is my privilege to present the first commemorative history book for the Waukegan Fire Department. Our department is rich with pride, tradition and a commitment to serve our community.

This book is dedicated to all Waukegan Firefighters past and present that have served the department and our city. Everything that we have achieved as a public safety agency can be attributed to our members through the outstanding service that they provide.

We also sincerely appreciative for the dedication to service provided to the department by our civilian employees and telecommunications staff as they continue to provide essential services to support our Firefighters and Officers.

Special thanks is also extended to our families as they are the foundation for our success, and the Waukegan City Council both past and present as their support of public safety has been remarkable over the years.

With 158 years of historical information, we are unable to include every event, photograph, and newspaper clipping in assembling this project. However, I hope you will agree that this effort deserves a lasting place in your memory and your home.

It is our hope that other WFD history books will follow to capture the fire service heritage we obtain as we continue to serve the people that live and work in Waukegan.

Respectfully and Sincerely Yours,

Patrick Gallagher, Fire Chief

A Fireman's Prayer

When I am called to duty, God,
Whenever flames may rage;
Give me strength to save some life,
Whatever be its age.
Help me embrace a little child
Before it is too late
Or save an older person
From the horror of that fate.
Enable me to be alert
And hear the weakest shout,
And quickly and efficiently
To put the fire out.
I want to fill my calling
And to give the best in me
To guard my every neighbor
And protect his property.
And if, according to my fate,
I am to lose my life,
Please bless with your protecting
My children and my wife.

- Author Unknown

WAUKEGAN FIREFIGHTERS
IAFF
LOCAL 473
AFL-CIO CLC

The International Association of Fire Fighters has more than 2,900 affiliates. Established in 1918, the IAFF represents fire fighters in more than 3,500 communities in the U.S. and Canada. The 267,000 members of the IAFF are the nation's full-time professional fire fighters and paramedics, who protect the lives and property of 85 percent of the nation's population.

The IAFF represents city and county fire fighters and emergency medical personnel, as well as state employees (such as the California Forestry fire fighters), federal workers (such as fire fighters on military installations), and fire and emergency medical workers employed at certain industrial facilities.

Local 473, organized in 1936, currently represents 100 fire fighters and fire lieutenants. In addition to several community philanthropy initiatives, Local 473 has established itself as one of Illinois' top contributors to the Muscular Dystrophy Association through an annual golf outing and other fund raising activities such as Fill the Boot. Following 9/11, Local 473 raised over $78,000 for the families of FDNY fire fighters.

LOCAL OFFICERS			
Year	President	V. President	Secretary	Treasurer
1943	Wenck	Ullry	Lisr	
1944	Wenck	Mullner	Helquist	
1945	True	Mullner	Singer	
1946	Mullner	Poirier	Drew	
1947	Poirier	Wenck	Lehtinen	
1948	Miks	Courson	Monroe	
1949	Helquist	Garnant	Monroe	
1950	Drew	Dillow	Monroe	
1951	Grun	Zuraris	Monroe	
1952	Seannis	Lehtinen	Monroe	
1953	Milewski	Lehtinen	Wallin	
1954	Lehtinen	Musick	Riner	
1954	Lehtinen	Musick	Dicig	
1955	Musick	Donavin	Dicig	
1956	Hayes	Dicig	Evans	
1957	Pavelick	Taylor	Holm	
1958	Pavelick	Evans	Holm	
1959	Pavelick	Repp	Holm	
1960	Courson	Figeas	Niemi	
1961	Horcher	Koncan	Niemi	
1962	Hull	Mullin	Regis	
1963	Worth	Rules	Regis	
1964	Worth	Rules	Regis	
1965	Koncan	Wallin	Regis	
1966	Koncan	Wallin	Regis	
1967	Koncan	Wallin	Regis	
1968	Figeas	Hull	Regis	
1969	Figeas	Hull	Regis	
1970	Mruk	Wallin	Miller	
1971	Lynch	Zupancic	Regis	
1972	Lynch	Shank	Regis	
1973	Lynch	Perkey	Regis	
1974	Perkey	Hushour	Colpaert	
1975	Perkey	Carlson	Hampson	
1976	Perkey	Carlson	Hampson	
1977	Perkey	Hampson	Hughes	
1978	Hampson	Harvey	Hughes	
1979	Harvey	Copenharve	Hughes	
1980	Harvey	Ramig	Richardson	
1981	Harvey	Ramig	Young	
1982	Harvey	Ramig	Young	
1983	Young	Bouma	McNellis	
1984	Young	Nelson	McNellis	
1985	Young	Nelson	Preston	
1986	Young	Nelson	Preston	
1987	Young	Gardey	Schmick	
1988	Young	Gardey	Schmick	
1989	Young	Gardey	Schmick	
1990	Young	Melendez	Schmick	
1991	Gallagher	Melendez	Schmick	
1992	Gallagher	Melendez	Schmick	
1993	Gallagher	Scholle	Schmick	
1994	Gallagher	Scholle	Schmick	
1995	Carlson	Scholle	Schmick	
1996	Grane	Scholle	Gruba	
1997	Scholle	Saickels	Gruba	
1998	Grane	Saickels	Camarzeo	
1999	Grane	Saickels	Camarzeo	
2000	Grane	Saickels	Camarzeo	
2000	Grane	Nordgren	Camarzeo	
2001	Nordgren	Dania	Bunrock	Camarzeo
2002	Nordgren	Bunrock	Soler	Camarzeo
2003	Nordgren	Bunrock	Soler	Camarzeo
2004	Nordgren	Bunrock	Soler	Long
2005	Nordgren	Bunrock	Soler	Long

FILL THE BOOT

Waukegan, one of the oldest communities in Illinois, can trace its history back to 1673, when Jesuit missionary Father Pierre Marquette and explorer Louis Joliet came upon the tree-covered bluffs in the area along Lake Michigan settled by the Potawatomi Indians. Trappers and traders followed, building a trading post and stockade in the early 1700s. They called it "Petite" or Little Fort. Eventually, the Frenchmen abandoned the fort. The first permanent settlers came from Chicago in 1835. The community soon thrived with factories, stores and new residences. In 1841, Little Fort was named county seat, taking that title from Libertyville. Between 1841 and 1846, its population had grown from 150 to 750.

By 1849, the town had a population of 2,500, and was officially listed as a port with the United States government. With this growth, "Little" no longer seemed appropriate in its name. On March 31, 1849, the Village of Little Fort, Illinois changed its name to Waukegan, derived from the Pottawamie term for Little Fort, Waukegan.

Early settlers were attracted to Waukegan because of its port. Produce and grain from Lake and McHenry County farms was shipped via Lake Michigan to Chicago. The creation of the Illinois Parallel Railroad (now the Chicago and Northwestern) in 1855 brought manufacturing to the city.

With the community's rapid and extensive growth came the need to provide basic services to its residents and businesses. The town needed fire protection for its warehouses, factories, hotels and the many frame houses that sprung up along its streets. As such, the first volunteer firemen organized the Waukegan Hook and Ladder Company No. 1 on December 27, 1849.

The new company included 21 volunteer firemen, who manned a small hook and ladder wagon and fought fires with axes and leather and wooden buckets. The members furnished their own uniforms; the only compensation a volunteer received for being in the company was a rebate of his poll tax. A .25 cent fee was imposed on anyone who was absent from roll call or from meeting. Members of the early department were recognized political, business and social leaders of the community. The meetings were held at businesses or establishments owned by one or more of the members until a permanent facility was built in the early 1850s.

During its first weeks, foreman J.D. Davis led the company; J.H. Hill took over that position on January 7, 1850. The other officers were E.S.L. Bacheldor, 1st Assistant Foreman; William M. Case, 2nd Assistant Foremen; W.C. Tiffany, Secretary; and William Hallowell, Assistant Secretary. The company fought is first fire on December 11, 1950. The blaze was at the Kirk Foundry, a one-story wooden building at the foot of County Street.

Equipment and facilities were dominant issues in the company's early history. On May 3, 1850, a committee was appointed to determine the cost of a fire engine for Waukegan and to find a suitable building to house the Hook and Ladder Company. Two years later, on October 25, 1852, the city passed an ordinance that authorized the purchase of a fire engine from the City of Chicago as well as the purchase of 300 feet of hose pipe from Charles E. Peck, of Chicago. This led to the formation of the first engine company.

The style of Waukegan firemen's first uniform was adopted on August 11, 1853. It consisted of red shirts with blue collars, and cuffs, blue caps with gilt buttons and black leather belts. The style of trousers was left up to each fireman.

The company's first fire engine turned out to be a disappointment. The Regular Bucket Brigade #1, after running several trial runs, reported on October 5, 1853 that the engine would not be effective in an emergency. The report recommended that the engine be returned to Chicago. Waukegan notified the City of Chicago, by way of attorney, that the engine was worthless. The village directed James Wiseman to put the engine in good order. One year later, on October 20, 1855, Mr. Wiseman returned the engine to Chicago. That city returned to Waukegan the bonds that were used to finance the engine's purchase.

On March 13, 1854, the village authorized $825 for the purchase of a 32-man power fire engine from L. Button and Company of Waterford. The engine was delivered, along with a $32.50 bill of freight, on December 14, 1854. Later that month, the council approved the first payment on the engine of $275, which had been raised by subscription. At the same meeting on December 30, the council approved $50 payable to S.W. Dowst for six months rent on a building to house the company.

The first move toward the establishment of a permanent fire facility was made on June 21, 1855, when the village authorized $371 to purchase a lot from Joseph Wallon. At that same meeting, the council approved a warrant of $450 to give to William H.J. Nichols for the construction of a new firehouse on the lot. The hook and ladder and engine companies met jointly on April 7, 1856, and W.H. Hill was elected as the company's Chief Engineer. In 1858, James S. Barker succeeded Engineer Hill. Then on January 4, 1859, Horatio James was elected to fill Chief Barker's un-expired term.

Waukegan took its first step toward becoming a city when on January 23, 1859, the State of Illinois granted the village a special charter. An election was held on February 23, 1859 to poll the voting residents on the issue. The results were 407 for incorporation and 122 against. That vote officially made Waukegan a city, with 5.62 square miles. At the new City Council's initiatory meeting, it placed the matter of electing the fire company's chief officers in the hands of the firemen.

The city continued to be challenged to provide services and infrastructures to meet the needs of its growing population. A resolution passed by the board on May 13, 1859 resolved one of those issues. The resolution required all male residents of the city between the ages of 21 and 50 to furnish three days of labor on the streets and highways. A person could commute the labor by paying 75 cents for each day. All fire department volunteers were exempt from the resolution. This exemption threatened to create a shortage of men to work on roads as more men preferred fire service. In response, on May 6, 1867, the council moved that, "the committee on fire and water be instructed to confer with the officers of the fire department and urge the importance of reducing the number to the smallest possible number and still not impair its efficiency as the present condition of the roads requires all the poll tax for their repair."

On April 7, 1860, an ordinance was recommended that would create a fire limit, stating, "No wood building shall hereafter be erected". In later years, the City Fire Brigade would insist upon the building of firewalls and brick buildings in the dense downtown to prevent the spread of fire. On April 9, 1866, the department was divided into three sections: an engine company, a hose company, and a hook and ladder company. Along with the change, came the establishment of the position of Chief Engineer. C.G. Buell was the first person elected to this post and held it until 1872.

At the January 3, 1870 meeting of the city council, the fire department requested heat for the fire engine house. The engine and hose were freezing up and could not be used. The response to increased concerns about the adequacy of the city's fire protection, the city purchased a Silsby Steam Fire Engine, 250 feet of hose, and a hose cart. According to a later article in the *Waukegan Daily Sun*, "The engine was brought here and exhibited and tested the latter part of August, 1874, and was accepted Sept. 7, 1874, the consideration being $4,800 for the engine and hose and $300 for the hose cart." Unlike the engine purchased a decade earlier, this one stood the test of time. It was rebuilt in 1892, and was "as capable of doing the same excellent service in 1902 as its initial trial before Waukegan citizens." Also in August 1874, the city council settled on the Hogan lots on Washington Street for the location of the new engine house. On Oct. 5, 1874, the council approved the hiring of William H. Wright as engineer of the Steam Fire Engine at a salary of $125 per year. Then in January 1875, a new fire company was organized, consisting of nine pump men and fifteen hose men, to operate the old hand engine.

The debate over the fire engine did not keep the Waukegan Fire Department from coming to the aid of their brother firemen in Chicago. On October 8, 1871, residents of Waukegan saw a red glow along the horizon to the south. Soon after, members of the Waukegan Fire Department received a telegram from firemen in Chicago, asking for help. Volunteer fireman Fred Palmer, William Sunderline, Patrick

The bell was purchased in 1858 and rested on the roof of No. 1 Engine Company in the late 1800s.

Cunningham, William Wright, Harry Kingley, William Yager, George Ludlow, C.B. Kittredge, and Phillip Brand took a train to Chicago, arriving at the Northwestern depot to assist the flame-ridden city. It was also reported that the department sent a cart and 700 feet of hose.

The city was still growing at a rapid pace during the 1870s. The city dug artesian wells early in that decade. In October 1875, the council reviewed a proposal to pipe water from the artesian wells to fire hydrants and to build a water tank to be used for fire fighting. In June of the following year, the council appropriated $300 for uniforms for the men in Fire Engine Company #1. On Sept. 7, 1876, the Fire and Water committee authorized the laying of a water main on Genesee Street, south of Washington, to Belvidere Street. Since there was a surplus of artesian well water, the committee

On April 2, 1860, then unknown politician Abraham Lincoln was in Waukegan giving a speech at the Dickson Hall at Washington Street, near State Street (now Sheridan Road). During his speech, a fire broke out in a nearby lakefront warehouse. A reporter for the local paper wrote that as the flames rose higher in the night sky, Lincoln's audience drifted away to watch the spectacle. Soon he was speaking to only a handful of men. He abruptly picked up his tall hat, plunked it on his head and led what remained of the audience out to the fire. Legend has it that Lincoln joined the firefighters in their efforts to contain the blaze, ruining his clothes.

When Lincoln left town the next day, the city owed him a new suit. The *Waukegan Gazette* reporter wrote that, "This is deeply regretted by all save a few of the chivalrous Democracy, who seem to rejoice over the fact that the meeting came to such an untimely end."

recommended that water mains be provided to all parts of the city as soon as funds became available.

Further steps towards modernizing the department were taken in 1880, when the Fire and Water committee authorized the installation of a telephone to connect the engine house to the city engineer's residence. On April 3, 1882, the council authorized the Fire and Water committee to repair the engine house and city lockup. (At the time, the city jail adjoined the engine house.) In June of that same year, the council approved the building of a 300-barrel cistern in the cellar of the engine house to be used by the Steam Fire Engine.

Even as steps toward modernization were being made, interest among volunteers was waning. Few attended the annual meeting on January 10, 1882. On April 17, 1882, Chief Engineer Crabtree reported to Council that the fire

department companies had disbanded. The *Waukegan Weekly Gazette* carried an opinion that, "In a city of 5,000 inhabitants there ought to be one or more organized companies. The city has a large number of neat uniforms that ought to be gathered together and only re-distributed when companies have been well organized." An alderman suggested that a company of ten men be organized to be paid five dollars each whenever called to put out a fire. There were objections to this plan by those who feared that it would cause some men to set fires in order to raise their pay. As a result, three aldermen were appointed to a committee to develop a plan for re-organization. The debate continued for the next several years. In 1886 and 1887, significant steps towards the goal of having a paid professional staff was undertaken by the City. The Chief Engineer was added to the city payroll at $50.00 a year and ten (10) other firemen received $25.00 annual salary.

On September 7, 1884, the council had held up a bill to make water records until a map of the water mains and connections could be made. The clerk was instructed to issue water licenses for all parties using the water from the city's artesian well and have the City Marshal collect the bills. In 1888, a tax levy was adopted and $3,000 allocated to the Fire and Water Committee.

In 1889, Central School was totally destroyed by fire. At its February 4th meeting, the council approved the use of several church basements as temporary schoolrooms. On January 5, 1891, P.W. Cunningham resigned as Chief of the Fire Department and the council approved the nomination of George D. Wardil as Fire Chief. Chief Wardil presented a report at the council meeting of February 2, 1891 and asked for approval of a new chemical engine and another Hook and Ladder Truck. The report also asked for three full-time firemen and another five to seven men who would be paid a fixed fee for every fire to which they reported.

Notable historical efforts pertaining to early fire prevention efforts included a request from Dr. Norman J. Roberts on June 1, 1891 to erect a frame building at the southeast corner of State Street (now known as Sheridan Rd.) and Washington Street. The building proposal included a plan to cover the exterior sides and roof with sheet metal, while the inside would be "fireproofed". The council granted approval. Two weeks later, on June 15, Mr. Robert Dady brought forward a petition to build a frame building that would employ corrugated iron siding with a roof of tar and gravel in order to comply with a new city ordinance on fire proofing buildings.

The Waukegan Fire Department was honored for its outstanding service by the Bluff City Fire Company #1, City of Kenosha on April 1, 1892, while battling the fire at the Northwestern Wire Mattress Company, also known as the Simmons Factory. In this spectacular fire, the Kenosha Crib Company, the Baldwin Coal Sheds, and four blocks of lumber lying between the Lake Michigan and Kenosha's Main Street were wiped out. The City of Kenosha bestowed a large hand sewn weighted silk tapestry to WFD commemorating its appreciation for its response to a large fire which required

Waukegan Fire Department in front of Engine House No. 1 in the early 1900s.

The WFD paraded its new nickel-plated steam water pumper. On its first run, the horses ran away going down Spring Street hill and the pumper was badly damaged. However, with repairs, it continued in service for many years.

many Fire Departments from many communities in order to extinguish the blaze.

Following a disastrous fire that destroyed the downtown area in early 1893, the city council employed John A. Cole to prepare plans and specifications for a water plant and distribution system. On April 6, the council passed a motion to erect a powerhouse for the City Water Works. Shortly thereafter, it approved the purchase of two water pumps—one high duty and one low duty—each with a 2,000,000-gallon capacity. On Feb. 19, 1894, the council formally adopted the city's comprehensive water works system.

In 1895, twenty-one fire alarm boxes (numbered 3 through 27) were placed within the city, almost exclusively in the downtown area, including Fireman's Hall at 115 Madison Street. That year, Aldermen George M. Pedley, John W. Hull, and Ernest C. Alford served on the Fire and Water Committee, which reviewed the operations of the Fire Department.

By 1897, the Waukegan Fire Department continued its growth with the acquisition of a new hook and ladder, hose company, and first class steam fire engine. The water supply from Lake Michigan was pumped in mains that ranged from

six to 19 inches, providing water pressure at the pump of 100 pounds per square inch. There were 159 fire hydrants and 30 alarm boxes located throughout the city. The firehouse was equipped with a gong and alarm system, which consisted of two circuits, and more than 20 miles of wire with a gong and register in the engine house. Gongs were also installed in the residences of the Chief, Assistant Chief, and small bells were located in the homes of many of the firemen. There was also a telephone connection and communication from the street alarm fire boxes, water works, engine house, and at the Chief's residence.

An 1899 fire at the United States Sugar Refinery caused over $150,000 in damage. However, the most serious fire of 1899 occurred on November 4, 1899 at the American Steel and Wire Company mill, with damage reported to be over $500,000—an incredible sum of money at that time. A disastrous fire on February 26, 1901 claimed two lives at the Alden Organ Factory.

By 1902, the Fire Department territory included the six miles within the city limits. The alarm system included 33 alarm boxes throughout the city. The department's equipment

Daniel Gallagher with Bill and Lou.

Eddie Klinesmith with Bob and Doc.

included one Silsby Steam Fire Engine, 1,875 feet of rubber hose, 1,150 feet of cotton hose, one hook and ladder truck carrying 247 feet of ladders, chemical extinguishers, hand pumps, and the many minor appliances found "only in the best fire houses". Chief Arch MacArthur and Assistant Chief Sars O'Farrell commanded 13 men.

In 1904, from January 12 through 14, Waukegan hosted the annual convention of the Illinois Firemen's Association. Chief Sars O'Farrell and his command staff, including Assistant Chief D.G. Hutton, Foreman Richard Drew, and Assistant Foreman O. Stanley, organized and hosted the convention. Other department members who were organized and were delegates to the convention were: O. Stanley, Chris Conners, David Gibson, J.H. Jansen, J. Balz, A. Murray, Gene Hicks, Ed Webb (substitute), and Charles Jackson (substitute).

The fire alarm system was expanded to include 75 boxes. Alarms transmitted through the Illinois Bell telephone company lines and two-way radios in the fire apparatus greatly facilitated this change. These alarm boxes continued in service until 1952.

On June 1, 1906, Sars O'Farrell, in his capacity as Fire Marshal, made his annual report to the City Council and Mayor. For that year, the department had 66 alarms, with a total fire loss of $3,745, which was a significant reduction of the previous year's loss of $9,321. Mr. O'Farrell reported that "Cap" the truck horse was in bad shape and recommended the purchase of a new team of horses and a concurrent steamer. Other points raised in the report included mention of the

new bath tub added to the fire station, the need for stricter fire ordinances to address unsafe building construction methods, the near-collision of fire equipment with the city's street cars due to the street cars' unsafe operation, and a request to limit the use of fire hydrants by only fire department personnel.

The North Shore Electric Plant Fire (located on Spring Street across from the Northwestern Train Depot) occurred on April 23, 1908. The fire caused a giant flywheel to break from its bearings, which resulted in the death of Fireman John Hobart Jansen. Mr. Jansen was the first member of the Waukegan Fire Department to die in the line of duty since the department was founded in 1849. Fireman Jansen left a wife and four children at the time of his passing.

Merchant Policeman Joe Paddock also died in that fire. Fireman Balz and Captain Gibson narrowly escaped death or serious injury as they were near Fireman Jansen who was operating a hose line at the blaze when the explosion took place. Beyond his duties as a fireman, Mr. Jansen was also the manager of the Waukegan Telephone Exchange

On July 26, 1910, Fire Marshal Sars O'Farrell reported that the loss from a fire at Thomas Brass and Iron Company fire was $122,657, a substantial loss for that time. Also lost at the fire was the neighboring Durand Steel Locker Company.

Local newspapers were instrumental in recording the fire department's history. The year 1911 saw the WFD as the topic for numerous articles. On Jan. 7, Mr. L.O. Wainwright complemented the fire department on its excellent work while battling a blaze at his factory on Chestnut Street. On March

Fire fighting personnel, horses and apparatus on parade in this turn of the century image.

24th, 1911, the paper reported on the groundbreaking for the new fire station at South Avenue and McAlister Street. A March 29th fire gutted the J.H. Norlander building at 1112 McAlister Street, which housed a butcher shop and a grocery store. A fire in the Larsen building on North Genesee Street, which started in the basement, resulted in $35,000 in damages. Fireman Joe McLick, who also worked at the wire mill, was injured while performing axe work at that blaze. Waukegan's Commissioner of public property, Mr. Elmer V. Ortis reported to the *Waukegan Daily Gazette* on May 23, 1911 that he had received numerous offers to trade land for the site of the new Central Fire Station. On May 18, 1911, the *Gazette*

Members of the department pose for this May 30, 1908 photo.

WAUKEGAN DAILY GAZETTE

FIFTY-SIXTH YEAR.   NO. 97.   THE WAUKEGAN DAILY GAZETTE, THURSDAY, APRIL 23, 1908.   PRICE TWO CENTS

FLY WHEEL RUNS WILD

TWO MEN KILLED BY FLYING FRAGMENTS OF PONDEROUS WHEEL

FIRE ACCIDENT WHICH DESTROYED NO. SHORE ELECTRIC PLANT

J. H. Jansen, Manager of the Chicago Telephone Company and One of City Firemen Killed While Fighting the Blaze—Merchant Policeman Joe Paddock the Second Victim—Terrible Accident Wednesday.   Absence of Power Prevented Operation of Many Small Factories, Delayed Newspapers, Etc.

SCENE OF WRECKED BUILDING.

FIREMAN VICTIM PROMINENT MAN; HIGHLY REGARDED

On April 23, 1908, the Waukegan Daily Gazette reported on the fire in which fireman J.H. Jansen lost his life. Jansen was the first fireman who lost his life in the line of duty for the Waukegan Fire Department.

Lou and Bill pose with fellow firefighters at the corner of Broadway and Sheridan Road.

Department members stand beside an early motor driven fire engine.

Fire fighters pose in front of the South Side Station (McAlister Street).

reported that Chiefs Hutton and O'Farrell had tapped firemen Gray and Webb as the new Captains of the Southside and Central Fire Stations. On May 31, 1911, the *Gazette* reported that the Chief of Police had offered a $10 reward for information leading to the arrest of a false alarm "fiend" which caused the fire department to respond to six false alarms from designated fire alarm boxes over a six day period. Chief Sars O'Farrell confirmed the mischievous behavior.

The first motor driven fire engine sped over some of Waukegan's unpaved streets in 1912, sometimes having to utilize chains on hard rubber tires to navigate snowy and muddy roadways.

The Central Fire Station was remodeled that same year, and officially dedicated on January 27, 1913. It had developed into a social center for the community. Residents gathered to watch the firemen respond to alarms.

Manufacturers Terminal burned on May 2, 1918. As a result of the damages caused by this fire, the federal government demanded that the city develop a fire protection system.

As reported in the *Waukegan Daily Sun*, Fireman Julius E. Schoenke died from pneumonia on May 3, 1928 after a very lengthy hospitalization. He was 34 when he died. Three years earlier, Fireman Schoenke had sustained a fractured leg when he was thrown from his fire truck in an accident at Belvidere and Genesee Street. Fireman Schoenke was a 10-year veteran of the department. His wife, the former Signe Moberg, was a maternal aunt to one of Waukegan's more famous natives, the writer Ray Bradbury.

Lou (left) and Bill, WFD fire horses, strut in the 1916 Waukegan Day Parade. On board were (from left to right): Driver E.C. Ullrey; Victor Swchultz, Clarence Webb, and Dodie Balz.

The American LaFrance truck and pumper at Central Station, 113 Madison St.

City officials joined members of the WFD at the dedication of Central Fire Station on January 27, 1913. Front row, seated from left to right: Commissioner Carl Atterberry, Commissioner, DO E.V. Orvis, City Attorney Arthur Bulkley, Assistant Fire Chief Hutton, Mr. Webb, Bob Smart (of the Streets Department), John Skene, Dan Gallagher with Bobby the department mascot, Pete Needham, Mr. Klinesmith, and Dody Balz. Back row, seated: Mayor Bidinger. Back row, standing from left to right: Commissioner Jake Dietmeyer, Commissioner Clarence W. Diver, Treasurer Theo H. Durst, Chief Sars O'Farrell, Arthur Goode, John Klema, Mr. Mason, Mr. Nimsgren, Police Magistrate Walt Taylor (at end of row).

WAUKEGAN FIRE DEPARTMENT 1922-23

SARS O'FARRELL
Chief

D. A. HUTTON
Assistant Chief

H. A. GRAY
Captain

A. MUNSON
Captain

R. NIMSGERN
Driver

GEO. NEEDHAM
Driver

A FRANCKE
Driver

O. THOMAS
Truckman

T. McNAMARA
Driver

GEO. RYCKMAN
Driver

JAS. FALLON
Pipeman

W. WORTH
Driver

A. NORMAN
Pipeman

J. SCHOENKE
Pipeman

D. GALLAGHER
Pipeman

E. KLINESMITH
Pipeman

JOS. BUSH
Pipeman

E. ULLREY
Pipeman

J. V. BALZ
Call Man

The members of the 1922-23 Waukegan Fire Department were led by Chief Sars O'Farrell.

1930s and 1940s

The 1930s and 1940s brought new challenges to the Waukegan Fire Department, as Waukegan struggled first with the economic difficulties of the Depression and later saw its resources challenged during wartime. Despite these difficulties, the department continued to be an innovator. In 1935, the Waukegan Fire Department pioneered inhalator-resuscitator work, in addition to traditional fire service duties. On June 26, 1936, the firemen joined the International Association of Firefighters and were issued the charter as IAFF Local 473.

Another serious fire occurred on December 16, 1943 that destroyed a portion of the east side of the one hundred block of North Genesee Street. Later, the Hein's Store would be built on this site.

The 1931 Annual Firemen's Banquet.

The Waukegan Fire Department (circa 1940s) were: (first row, left to right) Chief George Ryckman, Captain William Worth, Sr., Lieutenant Howard Garnant, Mechanic Hugo Gurn, Lieutenant Charles Gavigan, Walter Franke, Captain Daniel Poirier, Alarm Man Anthon Miks, Lieutenant Carl Hellquist, and Lieutenant Theodore Singer; (second row, left to right) Ray Woertz, Thomas Drew, Heimo Lehtenen, Edward Manonian, Robert True, Louis Mullner, Walter Hutton, Jr., George Courson, Theodore Stanulis, and Walter Monroe; (third row, left to right) Earl Dillow, William Donovan, George Opitz, Edward Brozie, Louis Milewski, Earlin Sandelin, Donald Klem, William Worth, Jr., and John Zuraitis.

Waukegan Lighthouse Fire

Lieutenant Daniel Poirier was joined by his four sons, James, Donald, Daniel and Kenneth for Christmas for their first Christmas together after World War II. All four men served during the war.

Chief Walter Hutton, 1944.

Engine Company No. 2.

The department acquired its first grass fire rig (#725) in the 1940s.

Waukegan Firemen; Walter Monroe, Assistant Chief Walter Hutton, and Anton Miks, plan for the 1949 Firemen's Ball.

On March 3, 1949, firemen were called to a residential fire at 523 North Avenue.

The aftermath of a fire at the Salvation Army, at the southeast corner of Sheridan Road and Water.

A fire occurred at the northeast corner of Genesee and Madison in 1947.

Fire Fighter Jim Asma leaps into life net during training.

1950s and 1960s

The post war boom brought new growth to Waukegan and the fire department. On September 28, 1952, Mayor Robert E. Coulson, Chief Norman Litz, and the council dedicated the West Side Fire Station located at 216 N. Lewis Ave. An estimated 3,000 people attended the event. Also dedicated was a new $16,000 Seagrave pumper. Later that year, on October 5, 1952, Chief Litz unveiled the city's new Seagrave 85-foot Aerial Ladder Truck, which was purchased at a price of $37,000.

Central station remodeled again in 1954. Four years later, the building was deemed obsolete due to space restrictions, and hazardous in its location of fire lines that ran through the congested streets of the business district. In 1962, the Central Fire Station moved from Madison Avenue to the city hall with facilities that faced West Street.

In June 1955, the Old Clock Tower at the Courthouse burned. Shortly thereafter, a fire prevention ordinance established a dedicated fire prevention bureau for the department. In 1958, the Nitro Chemical Plant located at 740 Market Street was gutted by fire. Waukegan Firemen fought the fire in brutally cold conditions. It took almost 11 hours to gain control of the stubborn fire.

Three captains, 11 lieutenants, one master mechanic, and 46 firemen staffed the Waukegan Fire Department in 1959. The department's rolling equipment included two rescue squad cars, emergency truck, four pumpers, one 85-foot aerial truck, one 65-foot aerial truck, and the chief's car. Firemen were on duty 56 hours a week. Firemen responded to approximately 600 calls that year. Illinois Bell Telephone Company transmitted fire alarms through its attended machine-switching central offices in its fireproof central offices in Waukegan's business district.

In 1960, a fire at the Johns Manville plant caused an estimated $6 million in damage. Other notable fires of that decade include the Commercial Hotel Fire in 1965, two fires at the Piggly Wiggly Store in 1964 and 1965, and the Sahs Warehouse Fire in 1966.

In 1966, the department responded to 1,530 calls with approximately the same number of firemen and equipment as seven years earlier. As the city grew, so did its fire department. In 1969, the North Side Fire Station was constructed at the corner of Golf Road and Jackson Street. That same year, the Waukegan Tannery was rocked by an explosion and tremendous fire necessitating all available apparatus and manpower.

Chief Norman Litz visits a fire department exhibit at the Lake County Historical Museum in the 1950s.

Waukegan firemen at a fire at 149 S. Genesee on January 12, 1956.

Theodore Singer with unidentified lady and fire apparatus.

The aerial extended to 85 feet, with Dick Repp, Tom Koncan, and William Worth pictured from top to bottom. The new truck, purchased for $37,000 from Seagrave Corp, was delivered on October 4, 1956.

The City of Kenosha gave this silk to the fire department in 1892 in recognition of its assistance in fighting the Northwestern Mattress Company fire. However, its whereabouts was unknown until 1958, when Lt. Ted Singer found it in the attic at fire headquarters. Here, Lt. Carl Hellquist (left) and Capt. Dan Poirier hold the banner. The banner was eventually restored and is now on display at the Lake County Museum.

Captain Daniel Poirier and Lt. Carl Hellquist.

The WFD gave Santa a lift in the 1950's. Driver Ray Wallin, Tiller Operator Don Taylor and Lieutenant Walter Hutton (left to right) are pictured with Santa.

Top Row (left to right): Ray Wallin, Don Taylor, Charles Dicig, and Roy Hampson. Front Row (left to right): unknown, John Evans, Joe Bauer, unknown, Ronnie Moore, and unknown individual.

Pictured, from left to right, are Waukegan Police Chief Gerald Riley, Acting Fire Chief Russell Wendt, unknown, unknown, FF Mark Alto, and FF Robert Dezoma.

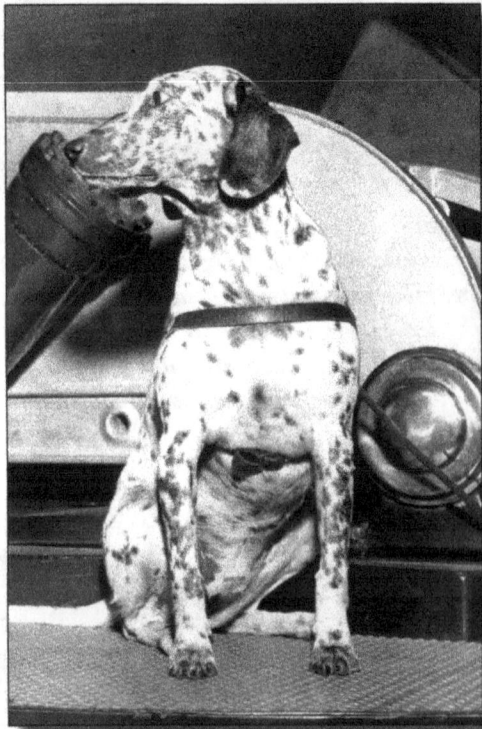

WFD Station #1 mascot, Lulu.

Above and below: Trucks line up outside the old Central Station at 113-115 Madison on January 9, 1962, the day of the move to the new headquarters at 105 N. West Street.

Fire Marshal Bud Ellis (Great Lakes FD) and Chief Norman Litz (right).

Equipment staged in front of Headquarters Station (left to right): Rescue Unit, Hook and Ladder #812, Engine #801, and Engine #815.

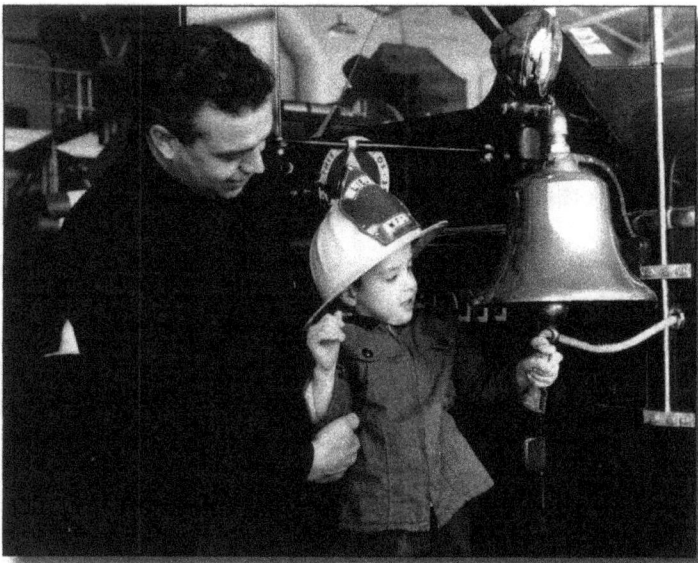

Fire Fighter George Hull and 1965 Lake County Easter seal child, Bobby Peterson, March 6, 1965.

Firemen hanging recruiting sign.

The 1350-gallon Ward LaFrance at the North Side Station on May 31, 1969. Pictured from left to right are Engineer William Worth, Chief Edward Pavelick, Lt. George Hull, Joseph Regis, and William Manning.

Fire Department, Foam Training Drill at wadsworth and 8th Street.

Chief Norman Litz (far left) and Firemen Hugo Gurn, Earl Dillow and Walter Monroe with the department's emergency medical equipment.

Firemen help out with food drive. Pictured (from left to right) Chief Theodore Singer, James Zupancic, Bob Ellis, Clarence Magnuson, Jack Stewart, Frank Turk, George Hull, John Strezo, Bob Liginski, and A.C. Walter Hutton.

West Side Station, 216 N. Lewis, in 1952.

North Side Station located at Golf and Jackson Street.

South Side Station in 1952 with the department's restored 1921 Stutz.

Retirees Edward Manoian (left) and James McGrain.

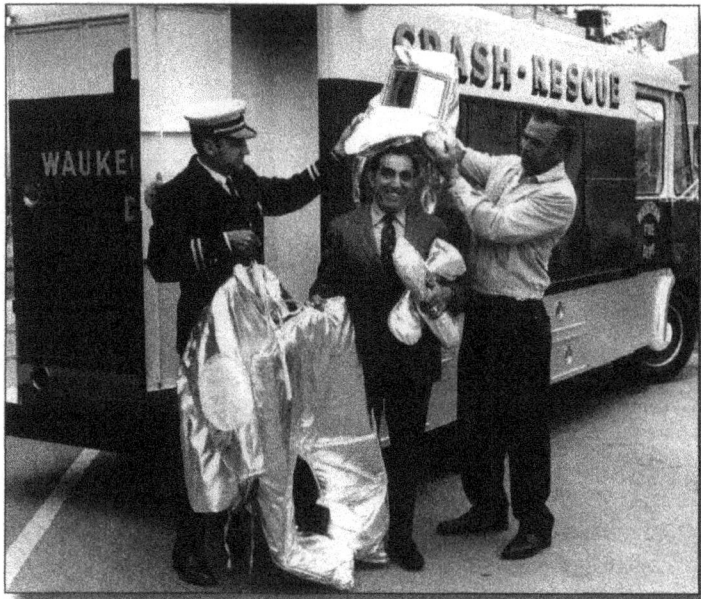

Chief Edward Pavelick, Mayor Robert Sabonjian, and George Hull.

Mike Storlie and Dale Adams examine equipment on January 11, 1963.

Tiller (Hook and Ladder) Apparatus, #812.

Polk Bros. Fire in 1968.

The department's newest pumper, which cost $16,000, sits next to one of its predecessors at the West Side station on November 4, 1953.

EVM fire on Water Street, Gebruary 10, 1971.

Bystanders watch as Fireman James Zupancic (left of) Fireman Ted Stanulis (wearing watch cap) aid accident victims.

Reverend Dean Ganster (front left) receives award from Chief Norman Litz (front right) as firemen (left to right) Theodore Singer, Russell Wendt, Erland Sandelin, and William Donovan look on..

INFORMATION
VISITORS WELCOME

Westside Station (N. Lewis and Monroe Street) mascot always willing to help station visitors.

Pictured in front of apparatus (Left to Right) are Firemen Hugo Gurn, unidentified, Carl Hellquist, Edward Monoian, and Ted Stanulis.

Griptous Hotel Fire, June 27, 1956.

65' Aerial Ladder Truck, #813, poised for duty at Station #3.

1970s

In 1972, Lt. Dale Adams established the Waukegan Fire Department Bomb Team under the direction of Fire Commissioner Edward R. Pavelick. Initial training for the new team was conducted by the New York Police Department and later through the FBI at the Redstone Arsenal in Huntsville, Alabama.

Commissioner Pavelick also established and introduced the first EMT-Paramedic program to protect the citizens of Waukegan during medical emergencies. The WFD was the second public safety agency in the state to offer this service. Waukegan's new EMTs were graduates of the first paramedic training class offered in Illinois.

In 1979, an unprecedented number of members retired from the department including Joseph Regis, Lt. John Kink, Richard Repp, Charles Ahlstrom, James Poirier, Sgt. Charles Dicig, Sgt. William Worth, Lt. Roy Hampson, Lt. James Hushour, Captain Louis Milewski, Lt. Joe Musick, Captain George Hull, and Jack Evans. These 13 members left the department with a combined 367 years of fire service experience.

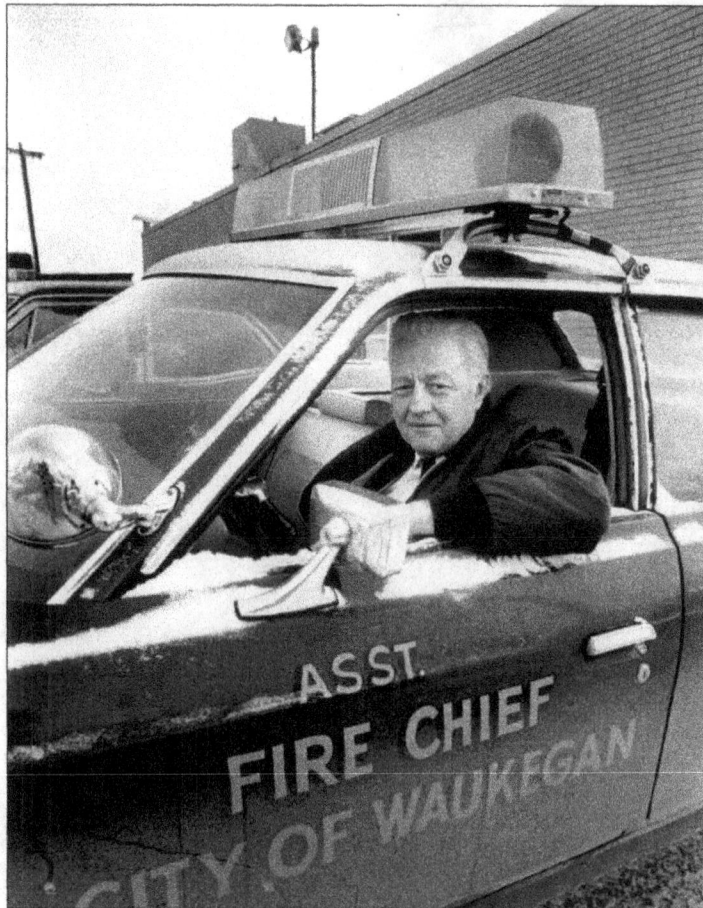

Assistant Fire Chief Walter Hutton.

Firemen promoted to Sergeant on November 24, 1970. Pictured from left to right: William Peacy, Joe Musick, John Kink, John Strezo, Bill Manning, John Pearson, Jim Zupancic, Reginald Satterfield, and Bill Figeas.

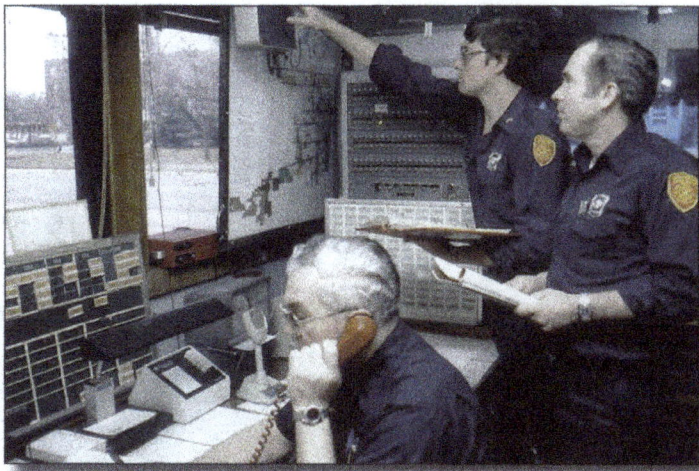

Duty Office at 105 N. West Street. Pictured from left to right: FF Donald Klem, Jeffrey Sterbenz, and Franklin Mercer.

Diver Don Knevitt

Great America's mascot Bugs Bunny with John Sherwood (left) and Michael Hutchison.

Tim Bratzke and Terry Persman.

Captain Dale Adams

Tom Sliva demonstrates CPR.

Fire Fighters sworn in as Lieutenant's (left to right): Bill Kirchmeyer, Eva Stuck (City Clerk), John "Jack" Kruse, Martin Da Vault, Ron Colpeart, Hugh "Buster" White, Daniel Simmet, Tom Berry, and Franklin Mercer.

16 recruit fire fighters sworn in on October 2, 1978.

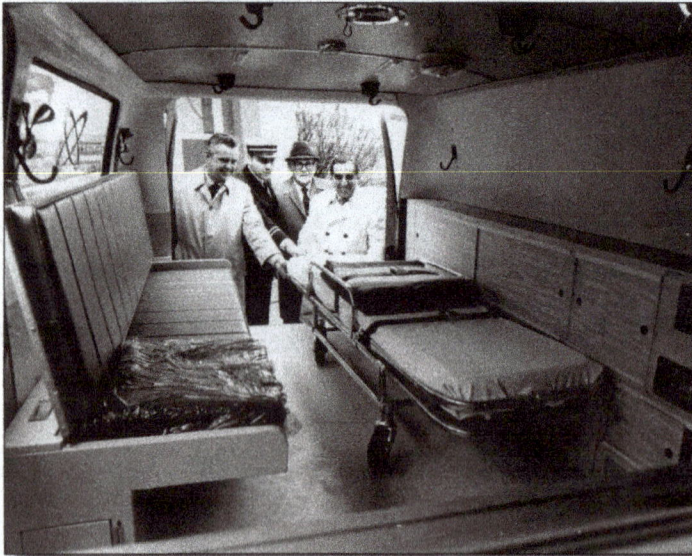

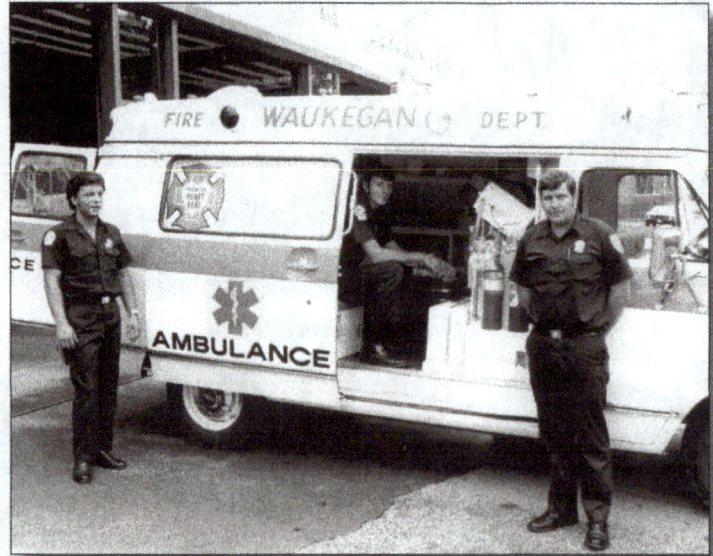

Above left: Noah Murphy, Chief Edward Pavelick, Mayor Bob Sabonjian, and Howard Guthrie look at the fire department's ambulance. Above right: Fire Fighters Jerry Koncan, Ron Colpeart and Terry Persman.

Tom Berry gives safety lesson to St. Anastasia grade school. Can you spot future fire fighter Mark DeRose?

Clifford Hook, Terry Persman, Tim Bratzke, and R. Ken Harvey (from left to right).

Firefighters responded to a plane crash at Waukegan airport on December 16, 1978.

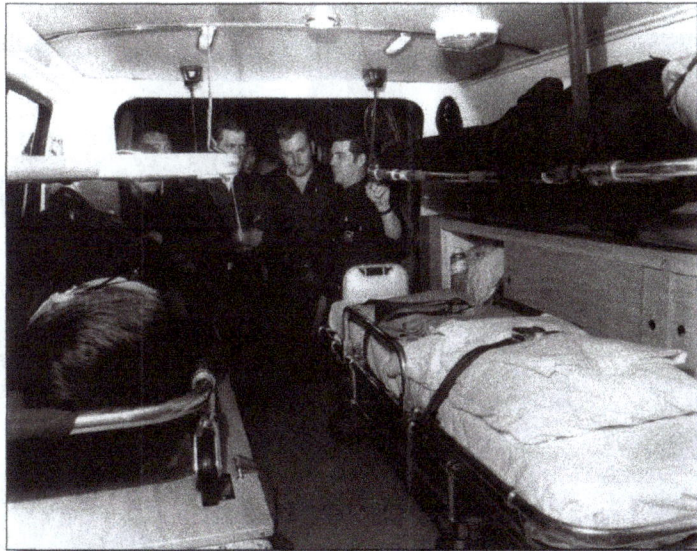

Mike Storlie, Tim Bratzke, and Donald Knevitt (l to r) look over department ambulance.

Tim Bratzke (left) and Lt. Dale Adams.

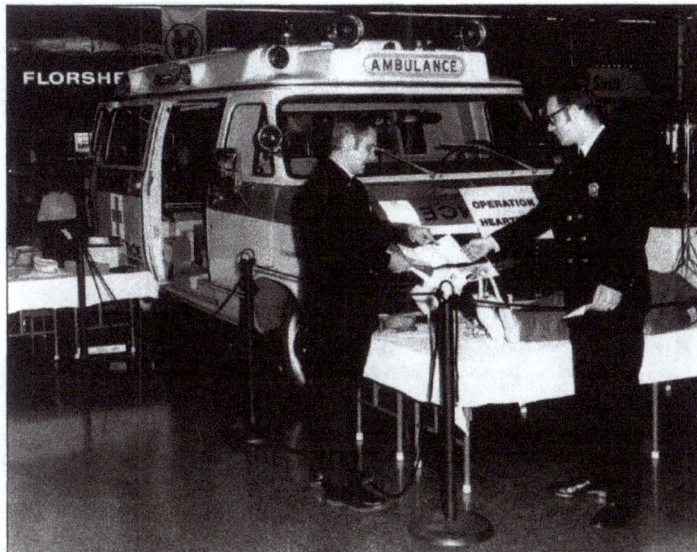

Firemen Dale Kilpatrick and William Rainey at the Belvidere Mall.

Firemen John Kink and Joe Musick (left to right, back towards camera) check out fire damage to a garage.

Firefighters inspect equipment. Pictured, from left to right, are Phil Sedar, Dennis Ostrander, Bill Figeas, Red Satterfield and Lt. Dave Dever.

Fire left Pierces Corner Restaurant in ruins.

Captain Jack Stewart (left) and Firefighter Bob Ellis carry a charred chair from the fire-gutted courthouse pub at 11 N. County St., on January 18, 1975.

Dale Kilpatrick instructs class in CPR.

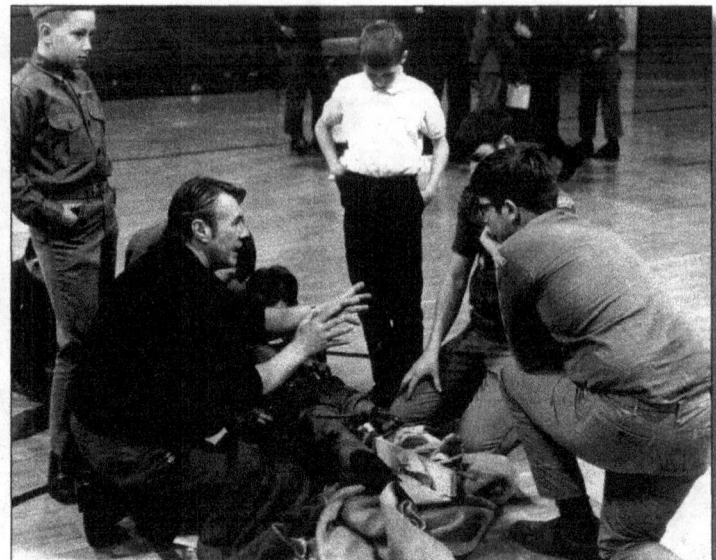

Richard Niemi describes fire department practices to school students.

Department's foam generation unit, Big "O".

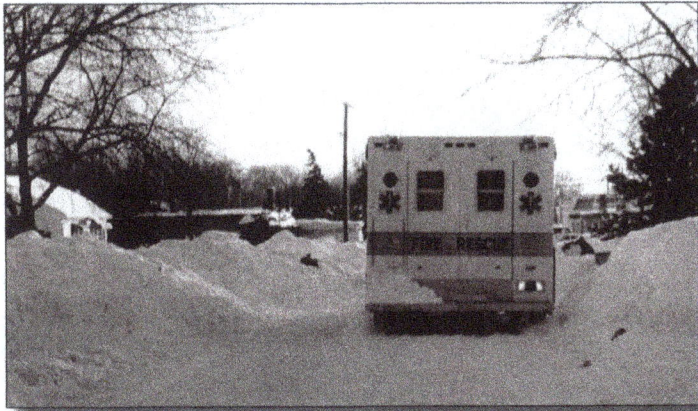

Rescue #824 proceeds down snow laden road during winter of 1978-1979.

Fireman James Poirier inspects extinguishers on Crash Rescue #819.

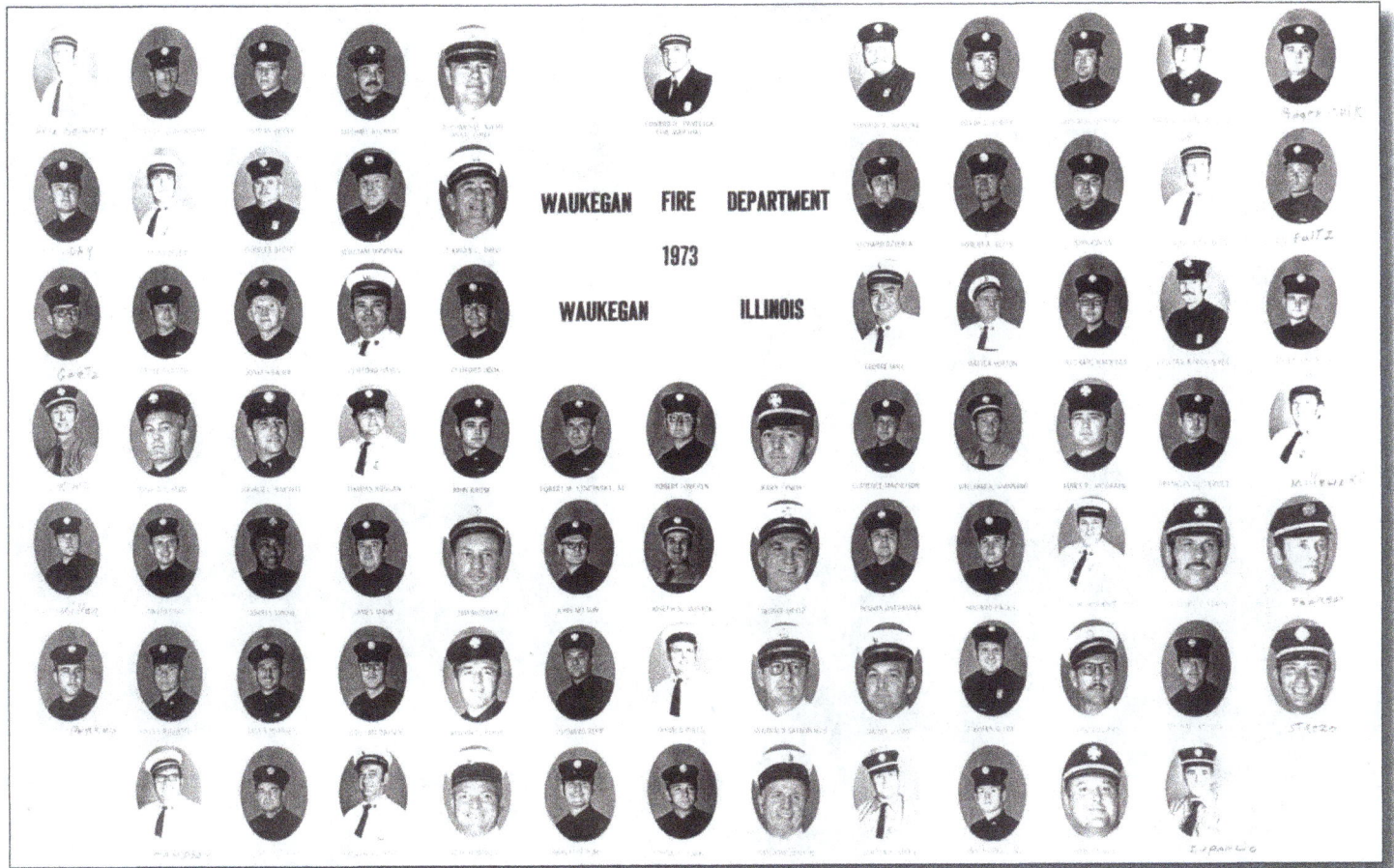

The members of the Waukegan Fire Department in 1973.

Santa and his team get a ride on WFD Snorkel No. 1.

Fire department members; Fred Tegel (left), Bob Liginski (center), and Harry Shank drill with foam at a training site located on 8th Street

Jerry Koncan and John Nelson ready the equipment.

Ready for flight are Tom Shafer, Robert Clare, and Charlie Moberly.

Fire department personnel are instructed by Lt. Dave Dever in Crash Rescue tools. Pictured A Shift personnel include: Bruce Grampo, Tom Miller, Jack Kruse, Jim Murrey, Phil Sedar, Tony Canelakes, Dennis Ostrander, and Bill Figeas.

1980s

One of the worst tragedies in Waukegan's history occurred when a fire began on Christmas morning 1984 at the Karcher Hotel on Washington Street, claiming the lives of nine people. Faulty wiring was thought to have caused the fire.

For the second time in our history, the Waukegan Fire Department mourned the loss of a brother firefighter who died in the line of duty. On December 29, 1985, Lt. Franklin Mercer lost his life while battling a house fire at 721 McAlister Street. Lt. Mercer had been operating a hose line on the second floor. Lt. Mercer joined his company in an aggressive interior attack after there was a report that children were trapped in the building. He died as a result of multiple injuries sustained when he fell through a floor that was weakened by the fire. At his funeral, representatives from 63 public safety agencies attended to honor his service. Lt. Mercer was survived by his wife, Paula, and two children.

In 1986, Chief Richard Kamerad established the "Vital Link" program to allow citizens and businesses to provide donations for the Fire Department's Paramedic program.

Right: Conferring (from left to right) are Don Pearson, Charles "Chuck" Perkey, Terry Block, Mike Storlie (in hat), Martin Davault and Tim Bratzke.

Pictured in the front row, from left to right, are Mark DeRose, Darnell Wright, Patrick Gallagher, and Ernie Rodriquez. In the back row, from left to right, are Tom Berry, Hugh White, Dave Roberts, and Don Knevitt.

Firfighters Tom Zelenz and Lou Milewski.

Lt. Robert Liginski.

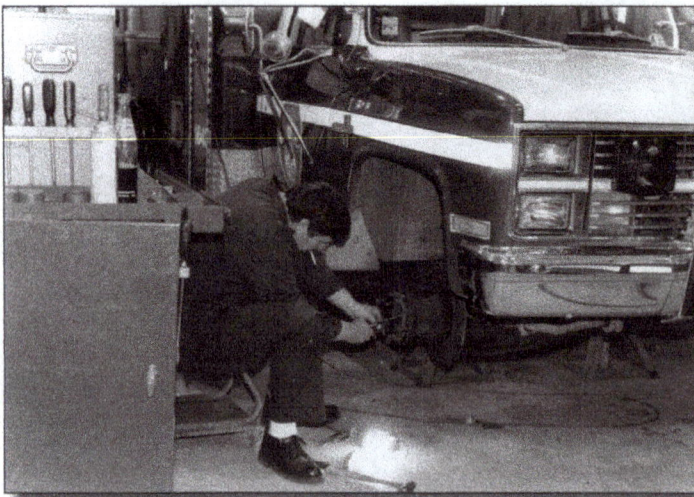
Fire Fighter Terry Persman fixes ambulance's brakes.

Bob Preston and Richard "Bo" Ramig.

Don Knevitt and John Zickus.

Bill Manning and Don Rules aboard the department's boat.

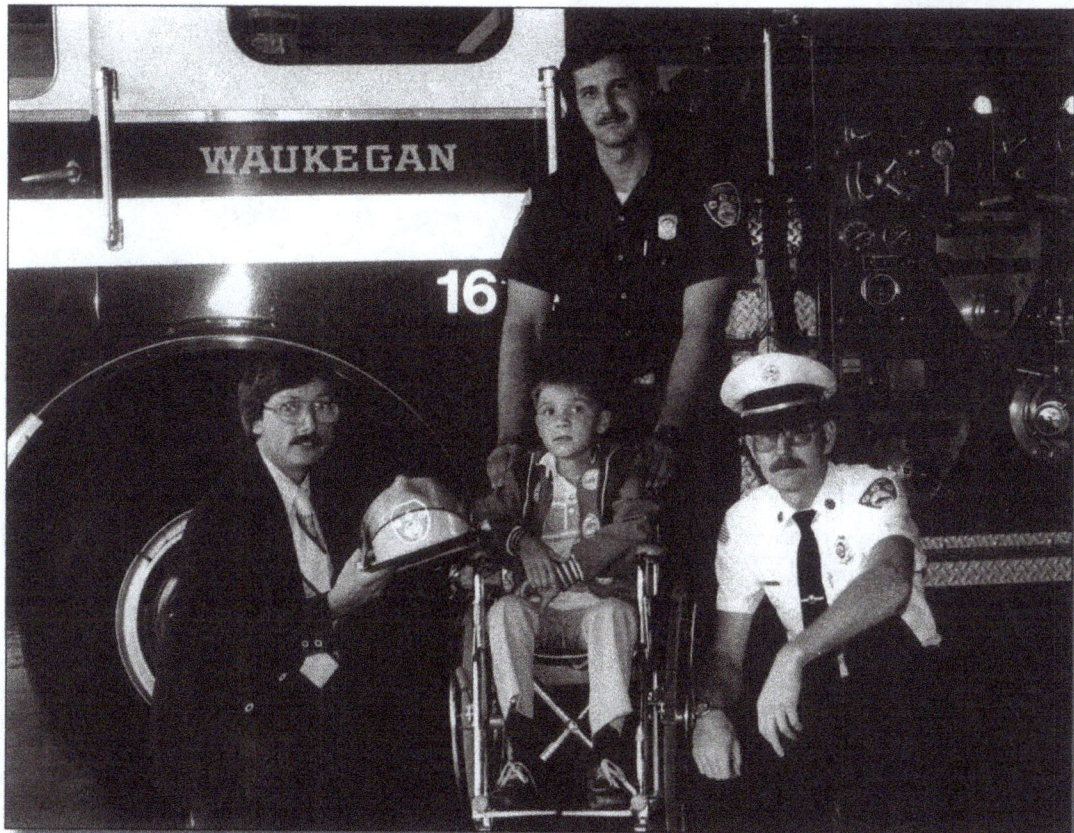

MDA poster child, Steve Marcelain in 1981 with Fire Chief William Peterson (left), Fire fighter Ken Harvey, and Assistant Chief Hugh White (right).

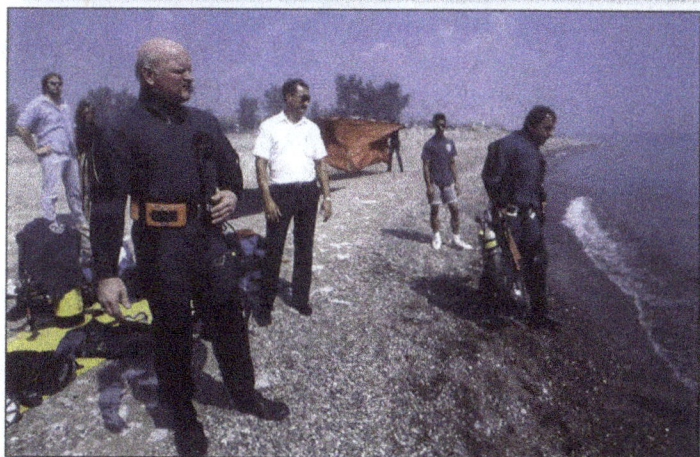

Robert Preston (left, in dive gear) and Chuck Perkey (right, in dive gear) prepare to dive while Lt. Howard Parks, (center, white shirt) looks on.

Lt. John DiNicola with fire fighters dousing structure after initial fire attack.

Flammable liquids class taught to students by fire fighters George Tsoflias (left) and Steven Orusa.

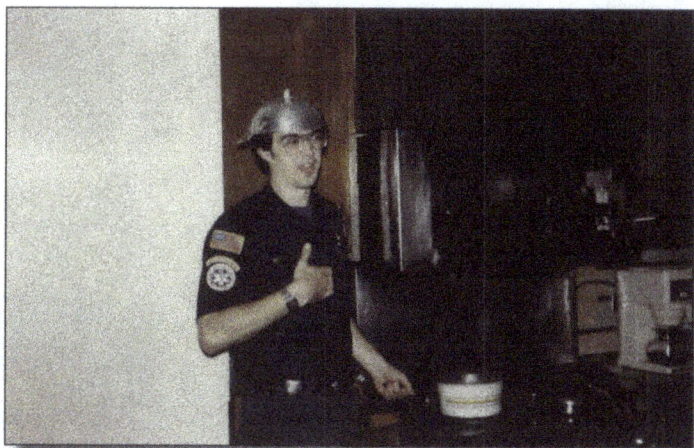

Fire Fighter John Sherwood and his tin man impersonation.

45

Pictured with Chief Hugh White (far right) are Don Barrett, Larry Zimmerman, Steve Orusa, Tom Zelenz, and Darnell Wright (from left to right).

Firefighter Bob Heraver rushes from a fire with a 6-month-old infant boy in his arms. The boy later succumbed to the burns he suffered in the fire. Six other children and a babysitter were saved.

Mayor Haig Paravonian (seated) dispatches emergency units while Fire Chief Rick Kamerad and communication empolyees look on.

1990s

In a spectacular daytime fire, the 96,000 square foot Waukegan Warehouse building was completely gutted by a maliciously-set fire on June 17, 1991.

Chief Charles Perkey purchased a new ladder truck and two new engines for the department from Seagrave Fire Apparatus Company in 1995.

In 1997, Chief Charles R. Perky, Deputy Chief John E. Terlap, Mayor William Durkin, and members of the City Council dedicated the new Fire Station #2 at 4505 McGaw. In 2000, the same administrative team dedicated Fire Station #5, 3221 N. Green Bay Road.

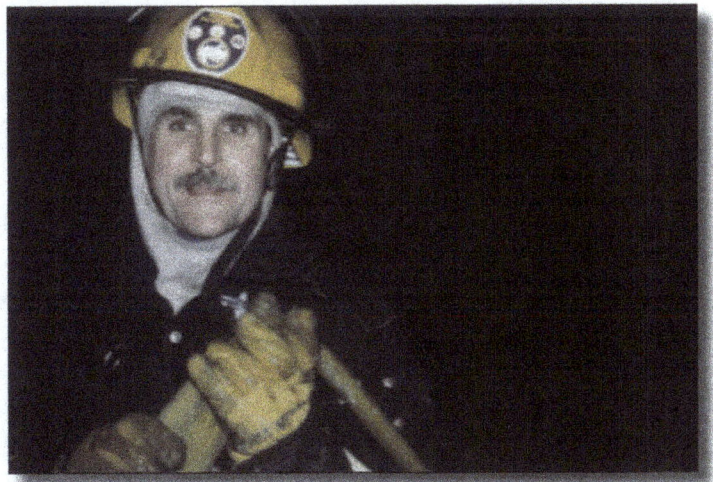

Fire Fighter Tom Shafer at work.

Engine #1633, a 75-foot Quint

Chief Dan Young and Waukegan Public School Teachers.

Lt. Don Pearson

Retired Fire Chief Chuck Perkey and Mayor Dan Drew.

Fire Department retiree James McGrain (left) accepts a commemorative IAFF flag in Lt. Franklin Mercer's memory on the 20th of September, 2003 from FF Jeremy Brown.

B shift Fire Fighters extinguish fire and then pose for photo. Front ow (left to right) Dan Kublank, BC John DiNicola (last active duty day), Lt. Tim Needham. Back row (left to right) Mark Pietraszak, Paul Rice, Lt. Mark DeRose, and Alphonso Ramos.

H and T Video Fire, 800 block of Glen Flora Avenue.

Waukegan's Dive Team and Safety personnel prepare for dive, (left to right) is Dave Paff, Laura Hedien, and Chief Patrick Gallagher.

2000s

On what will be known as 9-11, the department joins other city agencies in maintaining a high state of readiness by adding additional companies, and bomb technicians to protect the residents of Waukegan while the scope of the terrorist attacks was being defined. After the attack on the World Trade Center, Pentagon, and United Airlines Flight 93 on September 11, 2001, members of the Waukegan Fire Department attended memorial services in New York to honor those killed in the attacks. Immediately after 9-11, members of IAFF Local 473 along with other members of the department raised over $70,000 over a two-day period with a "pass the boot drive". The money was donated to the families of the 343 FDNY members who were killed in the line of duty.

In October 2002, the Fire Department of New York (FDNY) held their official memorial service at Madison Square Garden. Representatives from WFD were among the 55,000 uniformed firefighters in attendance.

A maliciously set fire at the Cub Foods store on September 3, 2001 caused $1 million in damage. Firefighter David Rigney sustained a fractured leg while performing assigned duties during the incident. The new Seagrave Heavy Rescue Squad 1 is dedicated into service on December 27, 2004.

On October 27, 2004, a hidden fire that went undetected for over an hour caused the total loss of the historic Academy Theatre. The Academy had begun as a silent movie house in the early 1900s.

The Fire Department received a new ladder truck from Pierce Apparatus Company. The truck is equipped with a 105-foot ladder, hose, and pump. It was placed into service in February 2007.

2007

In 2007 as this heads for publication, the 113 members of the fire department answered 9,407 calls for assistance, the most ever in our 158 years of history serving the residents of Waukegan.

Deputy Chief Steve Orusa, Chief Patrick Gallagher, and Assistant Chief Daniel Young at the Fireman's Memorial on 9-11-05.

Waukegan Fire Department's Command Staff and Fire Fighters pay respect to losses that occurred on September 11, 2001 in a memorial ceremony at Fireman's Park on 9-11-2005.

Firefighter John Carrier attends fire department public relations event.

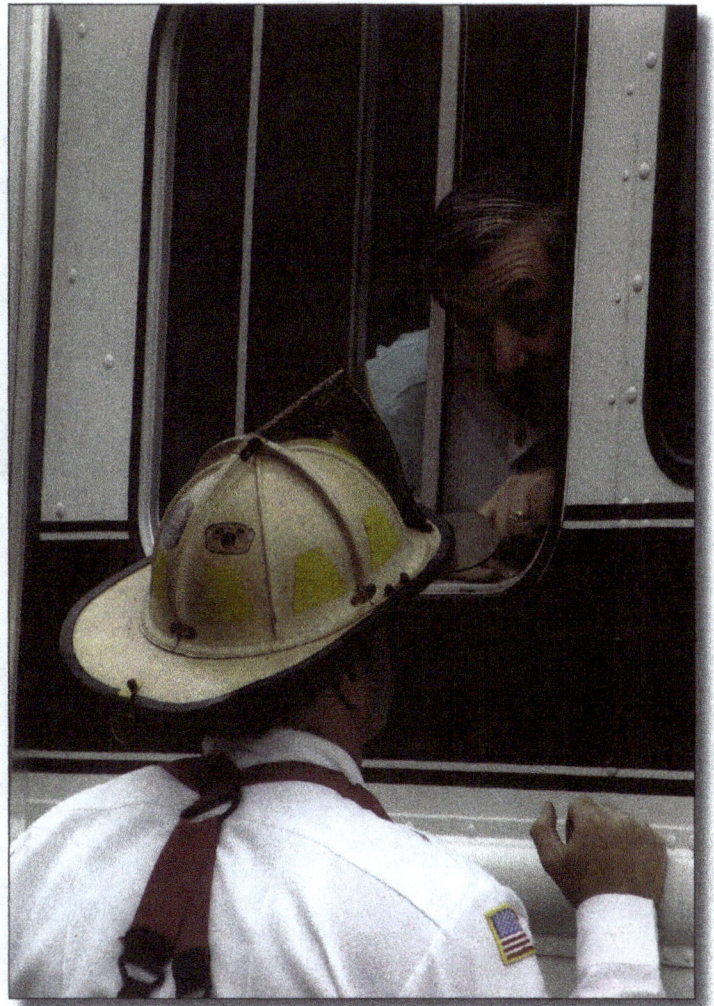

Academy Theater Fire, October 2004. Assistant Chief Dan Young with Deputy Chief Steve Orusa.

51

Pictured in the front row, from left to right, are Ken Mayfield, Joel Verbrick and Gregg Paiser. In the back, from left to right, are Dave Paff, John Nordgren, Eric Lyons, John Switalski, Paul Dawson, Jim O'Lear, and Deputy Chief Steve Orusa.

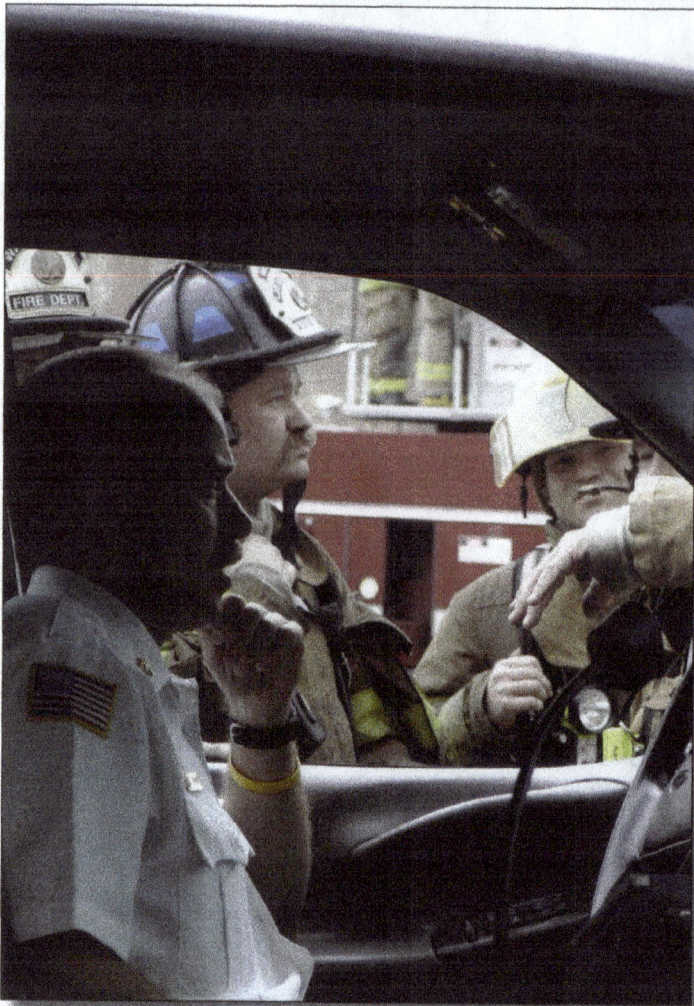

Fire Marshall Dan Young greets visitors at the 2004 Open House.

Battalion Chief John Schmidt, Lt. Mark DeRose and Kevin "Chomper" Oldham.

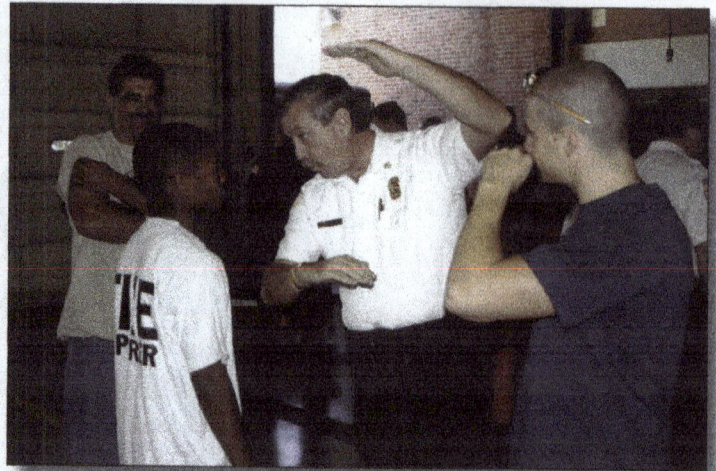

Matthew Burleson and Lt. John Switalski.

Retired Firefighters Dennis Mivshek and Howard Parks, seated from left to right. Standing, from left to right, are Charlie Moberly, Tom Shafer, Matt Salmi, Felipe Melendez, Tom Miller, Bo Ramig, and James McGrain.

From left to right, Jeffrey Welch, Steve Burkman, Joel Verbrick, Phil Melendez (retired), Captain Gene Decker and Ron Grant (retired).

At the Genessee Theater Grand Opening on December 3, 2004.

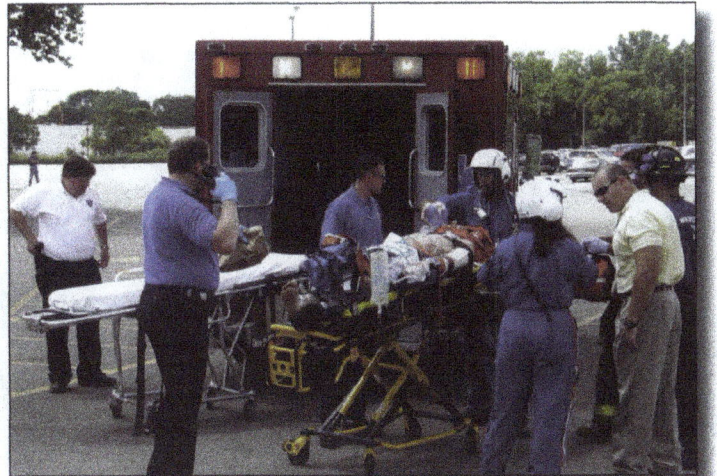

Lt. Steve Lenzi, Eric Lyons, Gregg Paiser, and Deputy Chief Steve Orusa.

Tom Shafer (retired), Darnell Wright, and Rolland "Richie" Richardson (retired).

Battalion Chief Ricco Farrell.

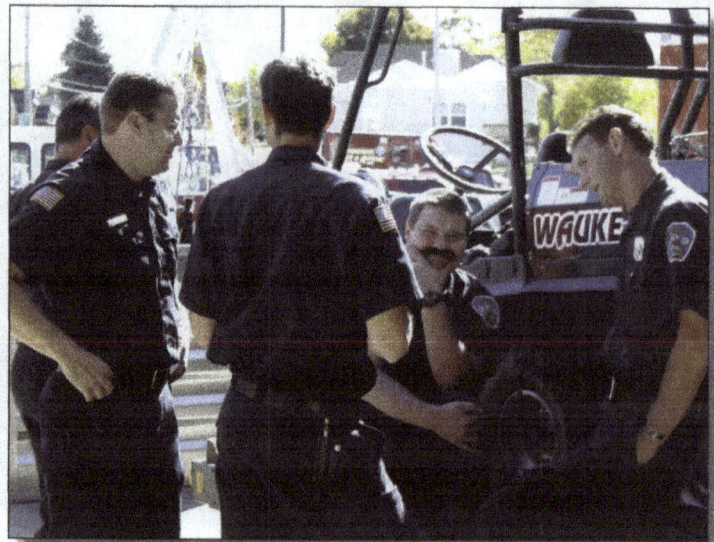

Personnel standing by for duty at a City of Waukegan Summer event.

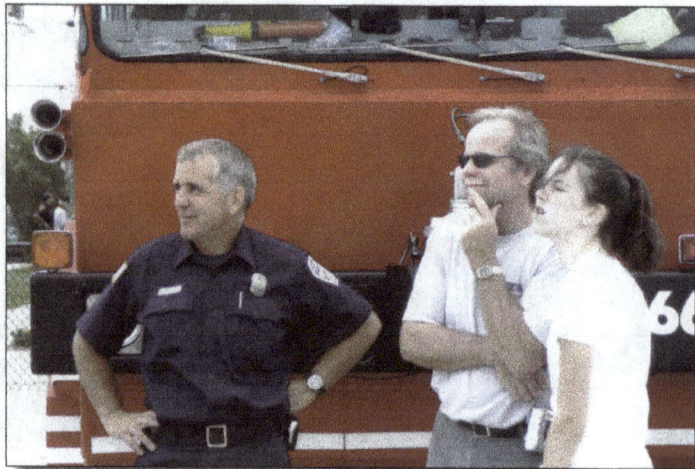

Tom Szostak and Pat Norton

Lt. Tom Christensen and Dr. Bruce Sands.

Squad 1 placed in service, 2004.

Honor guard members Lt. Dave Paff, Fire Fighter/Paramedic Damien McClinton, and Lt. Andrew Twombly.

Waukegan Fire Department
Fire Chiefs & Foremen

Foremen

J.D. Davis	1849
W.H. Hill	1850
I.R. Lyon	1851
W.B. Dodge	1852
W.H. Hill	1853, 1854, 1855, 1856
P. Edwards	1868

Fire Chiefs

W.H. Hill	1856
James S. Barker	1858
Horatio James	1859-1860
Louis Crabtree	1871-1882
P.W. Cunningham	1884-1891
George Wardil	1891
George D. Hardie	1891-1899
George Ryckman	1900
Arch McArthur	1901
Sars O'Farrell	1902-1935
Adolph Franke	1935-1937
Thomas J. "Buck" McNamara	1941-1945
Walter Hutton	1945-1946
George Ryckman	1946-1951
Anton Miks	1951
Russell Wendt	1951
Norman Litz	1952-1966
Theodore Singer	1966-1969
Edward Pavelick	1969-1973
Richard Niemi	1973-1979
Jack Stewart	1979
William Peterson	1979-1982
Hugh White	1982-1985
Richard Kamerad	1985-1993
Charles Perkey	1993-2001
Patrick Gallagher	2001-present

Mrs. Bess McClure

In speaking of our history, there are many friends of the Waukegan Fire Department over the years that have given time, talent, or just plain kindness to our members. We offer a special recognition and thanks to Mrs. Bess McClure, who over several decades sent letters, cards, and small gifts (great cookies) to WFD members. To recognize her kindness and caring for the men and women of our department, in 2003, Rescue 3 was dedicated in her honor. In later years, Jack Kruse, Jim McGrain, and Jeff Lynch who were all especially close with Bess, took extra good care of her as she did us. Following her passing in 2006, Bess was further honored by the members of IAFF Local 473 who established a scholarship in her name.

Honoring Mrs. Bess McClure are (left to right) Charlie Moberly, Donald Pearson, David Moll, Jeanne Milewski, David Roberts, Tom Sliva, John Bruno, Mrs. Bess McClure (front), Jack Kruse, Don Wochiehowski, Alderman Edith Newsome, Alderman John Balen, and Ray Vukovich, City of Waukegan Director of Governmental Services.

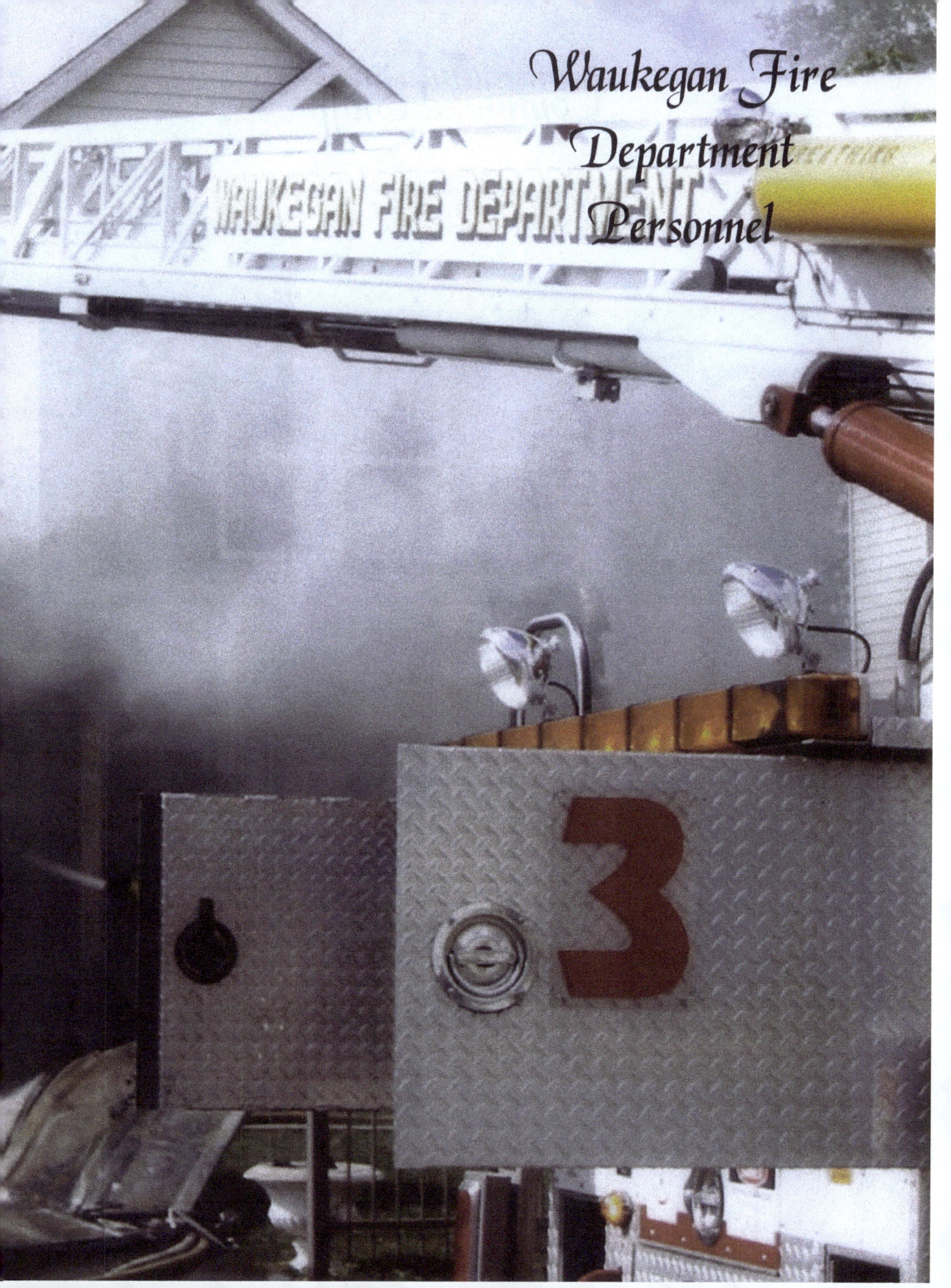

Waukegan Fire Department Personnel

Command Staff

Gene M. Decker
Captain

Ricco K. Farrell
Battalion Chief

Patrick Gallagher
Fire Chief

Jose L. Hernandez
Captain

Steven G. Lenzi
Fire Marshal

Steven Orusa
Deputy Chief

David M. Roberts
Battalion Chief

John M. Schmidt
Battalion Chief

C. Michael Scholle
Captain

Daniel A. Wright
Captain

Daniel L. Young
Deputy Chief

Active Staff

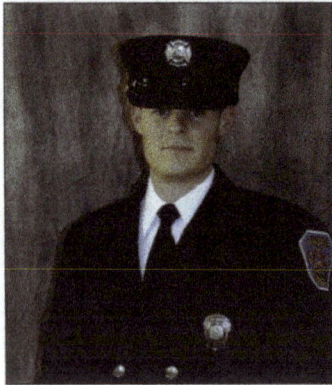

James M. Babb
Firefighter Paramedic

Eric H. Bakke
Firefighter Paramedic

Brian G. Bandel
Firefighter Paramedic

Sean C. Barbosa
Firefighter Paramedic

Lyle S. Bjoring
Firefighter Paramedic

Daniel P. Bordonaro
Firefighter Paramedic

Gregory J. Bozarth
Firefighter Paramedic

George Bridges
Lieutenant Paramedic

Daniel P. Brown
Firefighter Paramedic

Jeremy S. Brown
Firefighter Paramedic

Bradley J. Buntrock
Firefighter Paramedic

Steven A. Burkman
Lieutenant Paramedic

Matthew A. Burleson
Firefighter Paramedic

John Robert Calabrese
Firefighter Paramedic

Fire at Glen Flora and Lewis, fire fighter left to right: Reginald Satterfield (with glasses), James McGrain, and Robert Liginski.

Robert J. Callahan
Firefighter Paramedic

Douglas D. Camarato
Lieutenant Paramedic

Steven E. Carlson
Lieutenant Paramedic

John M. Carrier
Firefighter Paramedic

Scott G. Carstens
Firefighter Paramedic

Theodore N. Casper
Firefighter Paramedic

Thomas M. Christensen
Lieutenant Paramedic

Nathan Clark
Firefighter Paramedic

Fire Fighter Carl Hellquist rides on sideboard of 1921 Stutz.

Thomas W. Clasen
Firefighter

Steven G. Davis
Firefighter Paramedic

Paul F. Dawson
Firefighter Paramedic

Wayne M. DeLoncker
Firefighter Paramedic

Mark X. DeRose
Lieutenant Paramedic

Jonathan E. DiNicola
Probationary Firefighter

Elizabeth A. Eckert
Firefighter Paramedic

David P. Erdal
Lieutenant Paramedic

Steven M. Fedor
Lieutenant Paramedic

Christopher M. Ferguson
Firefighter Paramedic

David E. Freeman
Firefighter Paramedic

Michael S. Fudge
Firefighter Paramedic

Chad D. Gonwa
Firefighter Paramedic

Henry V. Gruba
Lieutenant Paramedic

Robert K. Harvey
Firefighter Paramedic

Laura E.A. Hedien
Lieutenant Paramedic

Kevin P. Heintz
Firefighter Paramedic

Lt. Henry Gruba (left) with fire department and Flight for Life personnel arriving for aero medical transport of victim from train accident, Yorkhouse Road at Northwestern Ave.

Robert A. Hutchison
Firefighter Paramedic

Peter J. Ihlen
Firefighter

Marcus G. Jackson
Firefighter Paramedic

Brian E. Jacobi
Firefighter Paramedic

Earle J. Johnson
Firefighter Paramedic

Justin A. Johnson
Firefighter

Michael S. Joseph
Firefighter Paramedic

Jeffrey R. Koch
Firefighter Paramedic

Chris A. Kohnke
Firefighter Paramedic

Mark T. Kolar
Firefighter Paramedic

Waukegan engine pictured with wild land fire in background on the Manville property.

Ryan M. Koncki
Firefighter Paramedic

John E. Kruse
Firefighter Paramedic

F.F. Melvin Pettis celebrates his last "Duty Day" with A-Shift Personnel.

Daniel F. Kublank
Firefighter Paramedic

Travis M. Larson
Firefighter

Troy W. Laws
Firefighter

Jack Long
Firefighter Paramedic

Barry Loyal
Firefighter Paramedic

John E. Ludford
Firefighter Paramedic

Troy A. Lynch
Firefighter Paramedic

Eric G. Lyons
Lieutenant Paramedic

Brian E. Marks
Firefighter Paramedic

Kenneth S. Mayfield
Firefighter Paramedic

Thomas W. McCarthy
Firefighter Paramedic

Damien L. McClinton
Firefighter Paramedic

Timothy R. McGrain
Firefighter Paramedic

Jacob C. Mount
Firefighter Paramedic

Steve S. Mudrak
Firefighter Paramedic

Timothy E. Needham
Lieutenant Paramedic

Jon E. Nordgren
Firefighter Paramedic

Fire suppression operations (Washington and S. Utica) during fire at the Karcher Hotel, December 24, 1984.

Patrick M. Norton
Firefighter Paramedic

James O'Lear
Firefighter Paramedic

Kevin D. Oldham
Firefighter Paramedic

David B. Paff
Lieutenant Paramedic

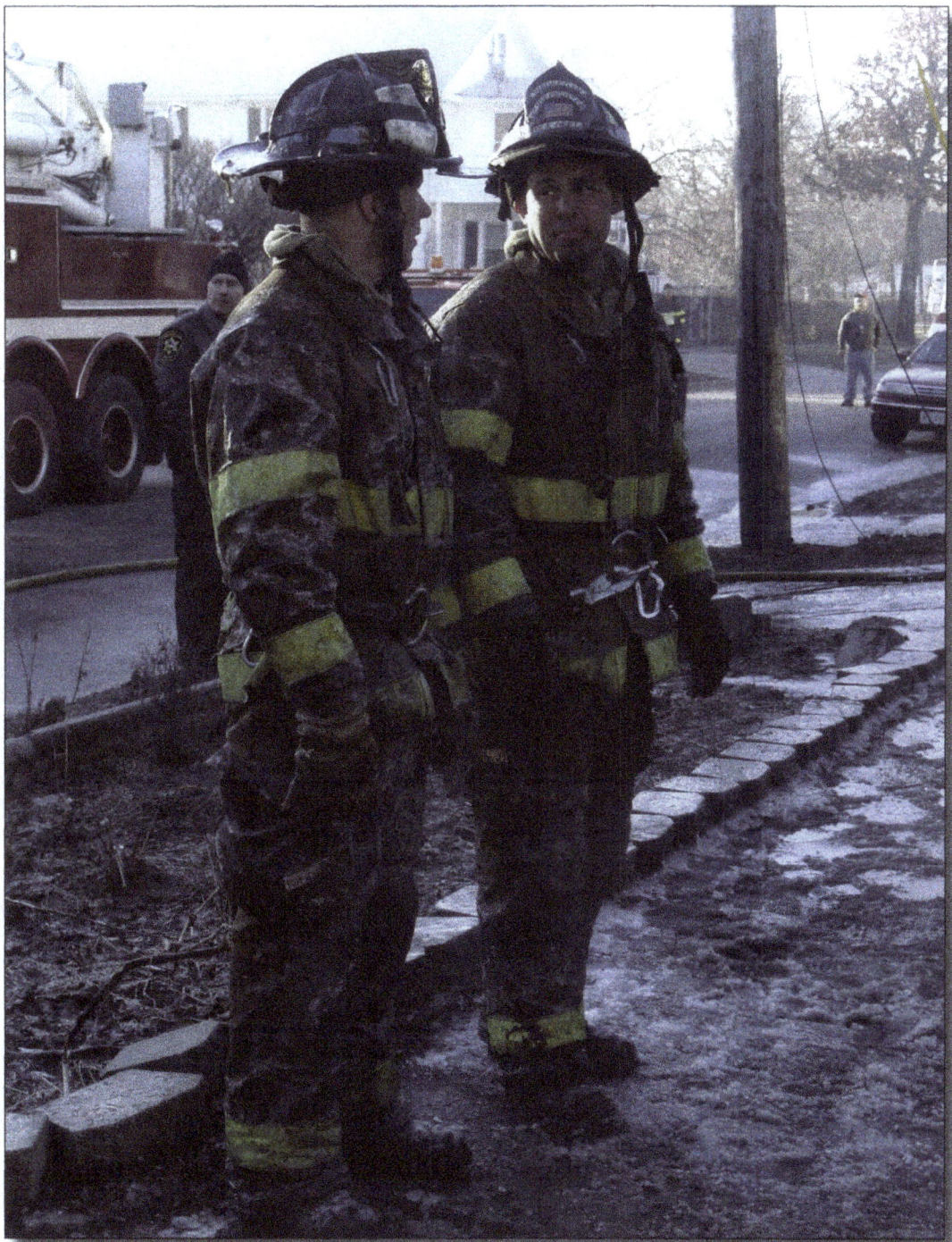

Lt. Joel Verbrick (left) and Firefighter Doug Camarato take a brief break at fire, 660 S. Jackson.

Gregg M. Paiser
Firefighter Paramedic

Mark Pawlik
Firefighter Paramedic

Donald Pearson
Lieutenant

Michael E. Pease
Firefighter Paramedic

Firefighters extinguish fire at 2681 Atlantic, August 23, 2005.

Mark E. Pietraszak
Firefighter Paramedic

Alfonso M. Ramos
Firefighter Paramedic

Brian G. Rau
Firefighter Paramedic

Scott R. Repec
Firefighter Paramedic

Paul A. Rice
Firefighter Paramedic

Thomas L. Richards
Lieutenant Paramedic

David M. Rigney
Lieutenant Paramedic

Daniel P. Romano
Firefighter Paramedic

Michael C. Schejbal
Firefighter Paramedic

Robert A. Schmidt
Firefighter Paramedic

Joseph J. Shaffer
Firefighter Paramedic

Nathan D. Skewes
Firefighter Paramedic

Adam M. Slade
Firefighter Paramedic

Anthony M. Soler
Firefighter Paramedic

Gregory L. Squires
Firefighter Paramedic

Brett A. Stickels
Lieutenant Paramedic

John S. Switalski
Lieutenant Paramedic

Thomas A. Szostak
Firefighter Paramedic

Lauralea Thomas
Firefighter Paramedic

Richard C. Van Horn
Firefighter Paramedic

The Bell Discount Center fire occured May 14, 1970, located in the 1500 block of N. Lewis Avenue.

71

Marco A. Vazquez
Firefighter Paramedic

Joel A. Verbrick
Lieutenant Paramedic

Scott D. Ward
Firefighter Paramedic

Jeffrey A. Welch
Lieutenant Paramedic

Michael Wintercorn
Firefighter Paramedic

Michael W. Wolczyz
Firefighter Paramedic

Greg K. Zahn
Firefighter Paramedic

Fire Department ARRF training drill (Oshkosh ARRF vehicle 1665) at Waukegan Regional Airport.

Thomas J. Zelenz
Lieutenant Paramedic

Todd M. Zupec
Firefighter Paramedic

Fire equipment and icy water used in fighting the Hein's Building fire litter the alley behind 122 Madison Street (looking north), directly across the street from the old Central Fire Station.

Support Staff

Ana Diaz
Clerical Tech - Level III

James R. Gardella
Public Safety MIS Coordinator

Charlotte Hughes
Administrative Assistant - Level I

Russell Nixon
Vehicle Maintenance

Kathy R. Pratt
Administrative Secretary

Lawrence J. TenPas
Fire Prevention Inspector/Civilian

David C. Ward
Fire Prevention Inspector/Civilian

Firefighter Dave Dever with orphans found under the porch at the South Side Fire House (South and McAlister)

Communications

Javier Arenas

Art Barnes

Lyn Batz

Tysly Brown

Denise Christianson

Nicki Coxon

Gina Gallegos

Sharon Gallegos

Irma Garza

Megan Grana

Jim Herring

Bud Hicks

Dawn Hilton

Daryl Jones

Rebecca Kumar

Dave Magnuson

Norman Marion

Brandi Mellenthin

Donna Monk

Angie Montemayor

Steve Nutgrass

Sue Rose-Sassone

Tonia Yancy

Fire Department personnel inspect the toboggan slide in Bowen Park.

Retirees

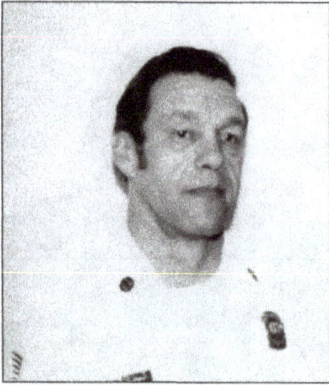

Dale J. Adams

Charles C. Ahlstrom

Mark Beeps Alto

Joseph Bauer

Terry Beaton

Richard Beck

Thomas E. Berry

Mike Bicanic

Terry Block

William R. Bouma

Tim Bratzke

Edward Brozie

John Bruno

Robert Burns

David Burry

Tony A. Canelakes

Dorland Carlson

Kenneth C. Cashmore

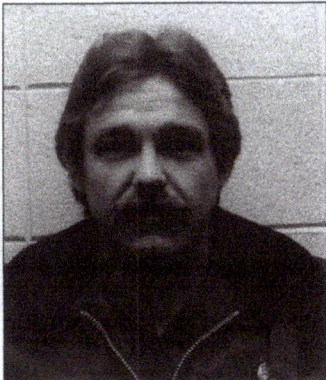

Robert Clare

Snorkel No. 1 drilling at the Tannery.

Fire Lieutenant John Switalski uses thermal imaging camera while Firefighter Steve Burkman douses some hidden embers.

Ron Colpaert

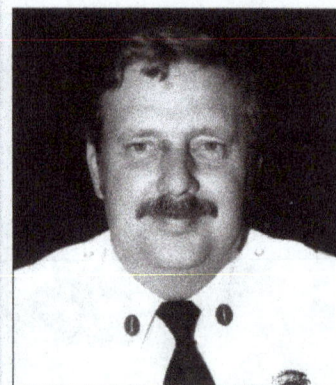

Randall L. Copenharve

Anthony Covington

Roger Cvik

Martin Davault

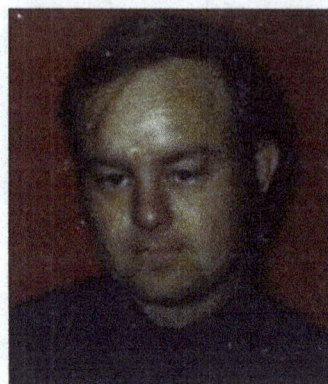

Charles Day

David Dever

Charles Dicig

Earl Dillow

John DiNicola

William Donovan

Thomas Drew

Richard Dzierla

Robert Ellis

Jack Evans

William Bill Figeas

David Foltz

Kevin Gartley

Donald Goetz

Joa Golec

Mass Causality Airport Drill, September 2004.

Bruce Grampo

Ron Grant

John Hakala

Roy Hampson

R. Ken Harvey Sr.

C. Hayes

Edwin Holm

Clifford Hook

Kenneth Horcher

Robert A. Hughes

George E. Hull

James Hushour

Michael Hutchison

Walter Hutton

Richard L. Kamerad

Dale Kilpatrick

John E. Kink

Firefighter Joe Regis is the passenger with his little driver on the 1921 Stutz Engine.

William Kirchmeyer

Donald Klem

Donald Knevitt

Gerald Koncan

Thomas Koncan

John Jack Kruse

Roy Lahti

Robert Liginski

Tom Liginski

Elvin Lovelace

Firefighter Steve Burkman investigates fatal fire at 660 S. Jackson Street.

Robert Lovgren

Walter Lucas

Jeff Lynch

Fire Department personnel wet down large apartment complex which was an estimated million dollar loss at the White Oak Apartment complex.

Clarence Magnuson

William Bill Manning

James R. McGrain

Mary McNellis

Personnel check out the view from ladder of tiller truck, West Side Station at Lewis and Monroe Street.

Franklin Mercer

Jeanne Milewski

Louis Milewski

Lou Milewski Jr.

Thomas Miller

Theodore Misiek

Dennis Mivshek

Charlie Moberly III

David Moll

Morris Moore

James J. Mruk

Thomas Mullin

Louis Mullner

J. Murray

Joseph Musick

John Nelson

Richard Niemi

Teamwork, Firefighters George Bridges (left) and Damien McClinton actively extinguishes fire at 660 S. Jackson Street.

George Opitz

Howard Parks

Edward "Butch" Pavelick

James Pavelick

William J. Peacy

John "Cliff" Pearson

Charles R. Perkey

Terry Persman

Fire personnel are instructed in monitor operations. Officers (Left to right with white shirts): Lt. Dave Dever, Lt. Ted Stanulis, and Assistant Chief Walter Hutton has a front row seat with instructor while others look on from street level.

Melvin L. Pettis

James O. Piquette

Subic Bay Lounge fire on Sunset Avenue.

James Poirier

Al Post

Kirk A. Preston

Robert Preston

Lawrence E. Quinn

Richard J. Ramig

Joseph Regis

Richard Repp

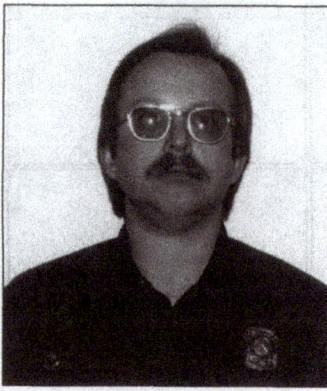

Rolland L. Richardson

Don Rules

James Salata

Matti Salmi

Erland Sandelin

Reginald "Red" Satterfield

George Scheiden

Lee Schluter

Philip Sedar

Charles Shafer

Thomas Shafer

Harry Shank

John G. Sherwood

Dan Simmet

Theodore Singer

Thomas Sliva

Ted Stanulis

Jack Stewart

Mike Storlie

John Strezo

Fred Tegel

Dwight Tenney

John Jack Terlap

Robert True

Frank A. Turk

Andrew Twombly

R. Wallin

Russell Wendt

Hugh H. White

Donald Wojciechowski

Willie Worth

Darnell Wright

John Zickus

James Zupancic

John Zuraitis

Scrapbook

Waukegan tiller truck, #812

B Shift poses for group photo.

Fire Fighter Jack Terlap engineering at fire.

Howard Guthrie, Commissioner Edward Pavelick, Mayor Robert Sabonjian, and Noah Murphy (left to right) pose with new fire department rescue squads.

Alderman Lawrence Ten Pas, Chief Patrick Gallagher (left to right) present fire department blanket to Mayor and representative of Waukegan's sister city in Japan.

Hawthorne Melody Farms provide team of horses to pull Waukegan Fire Department coal fired pumper (1958). Fire Fighter Howard Garnett is stoking the fire, rear of the pumper.

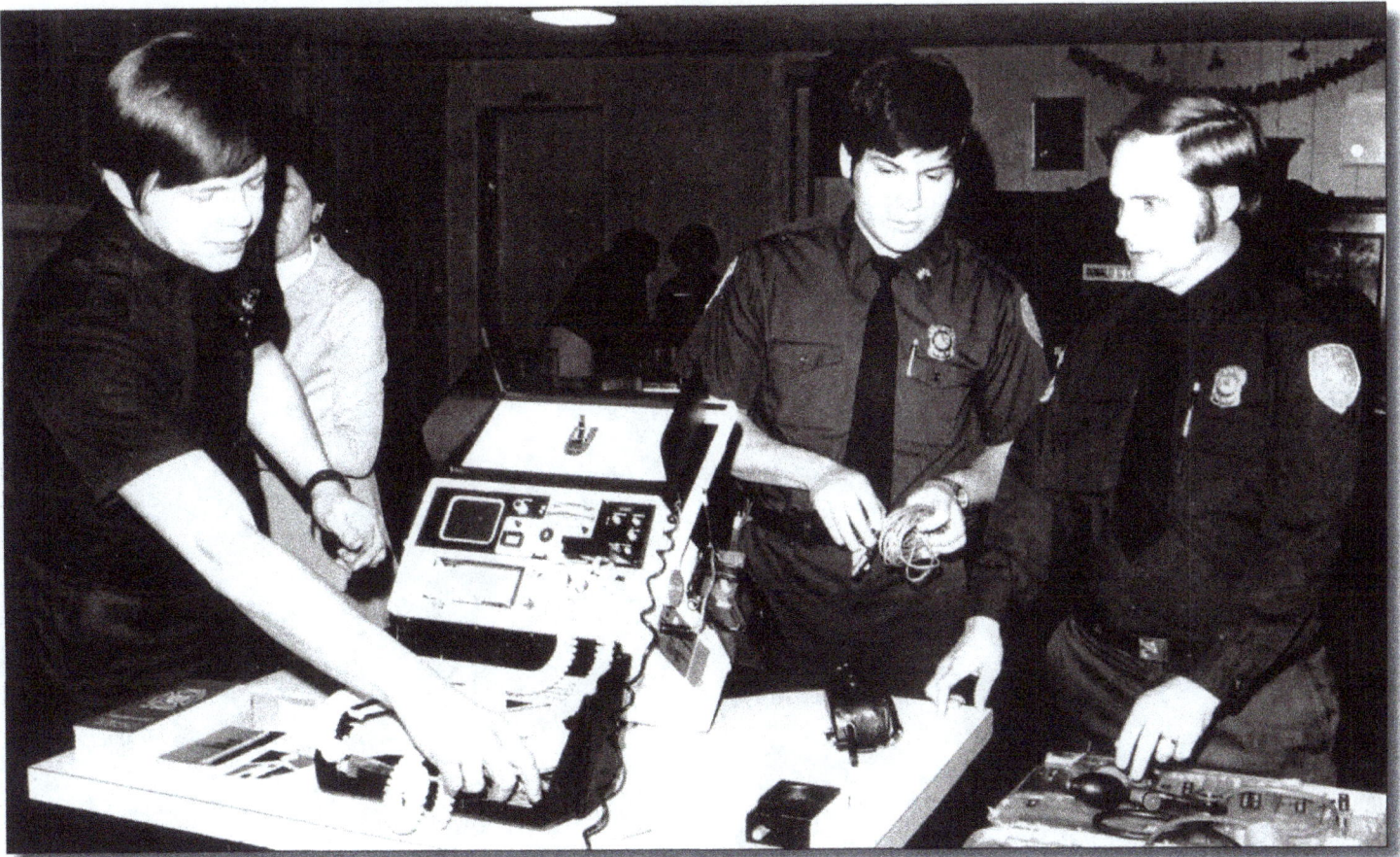

Fire Fighters Don Wojciechowski, Phil Melendez and Dale Kilpatrick (left to right) demonstrated paramedic equipment at open house.

Fire Fighter Brad Buntrock, Fire Fighter John Ludford, and Lt. Dave Erdal (left to right) at Station #5.

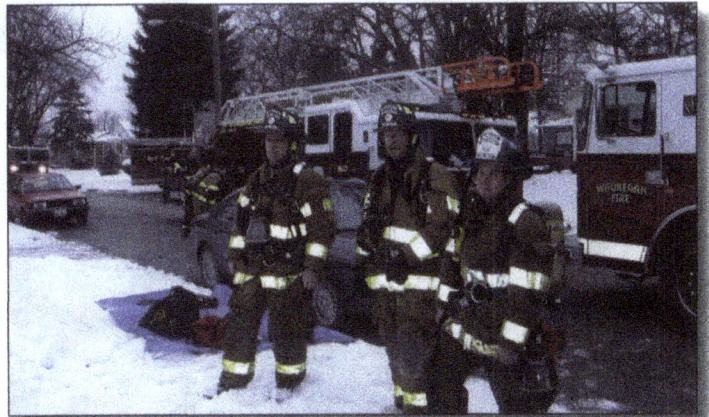

RIT Company members FF Tom Szostak, FF John Ludford and Lt. Tom Christensen.

Lt. John Strezo, Larry Quinn, Mike Storlie, Jeff Sterbenz, and Rick Kamerad (left to right) pose with Engine 813.

Lt. Steve Fedor, Melvin Pettis, and Mark Pawlick (left to right) at Station #2.

Fire Fighters Beth Eckert, Robert Hutchinson, Gregg Paiser, Doug Camarato, Capt. Mike Scholle, Capt. Jose Hernandez, Battalion Chief David Roberts, Fire Fighters Mike Pease and Daniel Bordonaro (left to right) staffing Station 1 (A Shift).

Left: Waukegan Snorkel #1 (814) at South Side Station #2, South and McAlister Streets.

Below: Waukegan Officers are joined by Mayor Richard Hyde (front) for photo next to Engine 1615 at Station #5. Officers (left to right) are Capt. Jose Hernandez, BC Ricco Farrell, Lt. Steven Carlson, Lt. John Switalski, BC Jack Kruse, Lt. Steven Fedor, BC David Roberts, Chief Patrick Gallagher, and DC Steven Orusa.

Restored 1921 Stutz Fire Engine in front of Station #3, 216 N. Lewis Avenue.

Right: Fire Fighters Pat Norton and Brian Marks (left to right) take a breather at fire scene.

Bottom left: Lt. Dave Rigney, Fire Fighters Robert Callahan, Jon Nordgren, John Kruse and Paul Dawson (left to right) man Station #5 (B Shift).

Bottom right: DC Steve Orusa oversees Fire Fighters Ken Mayfield, Jim O'Lear and additional personnel (left to right) with train accident victim at Yorkhouse Road and Northwestern Avenue.

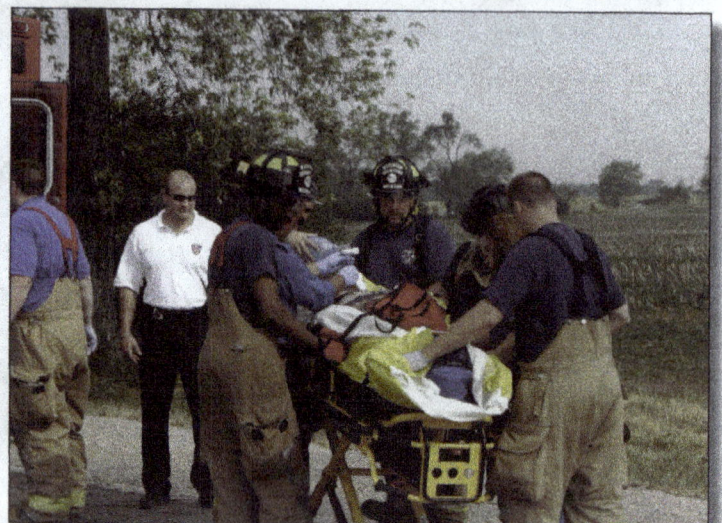

Fire Fighters John Strezo, Tom Berry, and Tim Bratzke (left to right) in bucket of Waukegan Snorkel #1.

Fire Fighters John Nelson and Tim Bratzke (left to right) work with the "Jaws of Life".

Fire Commissioner Edward Pavelick standing on the deck of Waukegan's 35' Fire Boat in Harbor next to Yacht Club.

Fire Fighters Clarence Magnuson and Jack Kruse converse (far left to right) during a fire ground break.

Fire Fighters Bob Preston, Richard Ramig, Lt. Freddie Tegel, Fire Fighters Roger Cvik, and William Bouma (left to right) pose for department photo.

Chief Edward Pavelick, Lt. David Dever, Capt. George Hull, and Fire Fighters Jim Poirier, James Houshour, and Richard Dzierla (left to right) pose for photo of the new Crash Rescue #819.

Fire Fighters Todd Zupec, Scott Ward, Krik Preston, Pat Norton, and Lt. Tom Richards (left to right) man Station #4, Jackson and Golf.

Fire Fighter Tony Covington, Lt. David Paff, and Fire Fighters Ben Friel, Adam Slade, and Earle Johnson (left to right) man Station #4, Jackson and Golf.

Mayor Hyde addresses firefighters and families.

Chief Norman Litz (right) pose with Mr. Win Reed (VP of Reed Randle) and 7th Ward Alderman Fred Burgess with new fire department ambulances in 1959.

Flight for Life is at the ready in field while fire personnel prepare to transfer patient to aero-medical crew for transport to hospital.

FF Ryan Koncki and FF Derrick Holland

FF Mark Pawlik and FF Damien McClinton

B Shift personnel manning Station 1. From left to right are: Fire Fighters Eric Baake, John Carrier, Dan Kublank, Lt. Tom Christensen, Capt. Dan Wright, Fire Fighters Tom Szostak, Chad Gonwa, Lt. John Switalski, and Paul Rice.

Left: Fire Fighters in action at 660 S. Jackson Street.

Bottom: Group Photo at Station #5, left to right: Bill Manning, Jeanne Milewski, Dave Moll, Mr. and Mrs. John Kink, Jim McGrain, George Hull, Mr. and Mrs. Joe Musick, and Gene Decker.

Right: Lt. Tom Christensen and unidentified fire fighter help during fire investigation at 660 S. Jackson Street.

Bottom: Fire Investigation of fire at Beatrice Foods, 2-4-1957.

Fire Fighters under direction of DC Steve Orusa work at a trench collapse on Waukegan's near north side.

Fire Department battles blaze at Whispering Oaks Apartment Complex.

Waukegan Fire Fighters participated in health and fitness competition in with other Lake County Public Safety professionals.

Ret. Chief Jim McGrain, Mrs. George Opitz and Mrs. Louis Milewski.

Capt. E. C. Ullrey poses next to Fire Department vehicle.

Fire personnel at promotion of fire fighters to officer rank. Left to right are: Chief Patrick Gallagher, Battalion Chiefs Ricco Farrell, John Schmidt, and John Dinicola, Lt. Joel Verbrick, Captains Daniel Wright, and Gene Decker, Lt. Laura Hedien, and Deputy Chief Steve Orusa.

Fire at the Dutch Mills Cleaners on McAlister Street, September 20, 1956.

Pictured left to right: Lt. Jim Mruk and Fire Fighters J. Daniel Spice, Gary Hampson, Daniel Crane, and Robert Hughes.

Waukegan Fire Fighter Ken Mayfield.

C Shift personnel, at Station #1, (left to right) Fire Fighters Ken Mayfield, Chris Ferguson, and George Bridges, Captain Gene Decker, Battalion Ricco Farrell, and Fire Fighters Steve Davis, Steve Mudrak, and Mike Schejbel.

Alderman John Balen (holding helmet) honored as Public Safety Chairman by Fire Department personnel.
Left to right: Lt. Steve Carlson, Lt. Tom Christensen, Mark Carrier, Tom Szostak, Dan Kublank, Ben Friel,
Chief Gallagher, Deputy Chief Steve Orusa, Deputy Chief Dan Young, Mark Pietraszak, Chad Gonwa,
Jacob Mount, and John Kruse.

Station 3 personnel, Fire Fighter Scott Repec and Michael Wolczyz (left to right).

Photo of the alley behind Madison Avenue Fire House in 1912.

Deputy Chief Steven Orusa, Captain Michael Hutchison, and Fire Fighter Jim O'Lear during action at a fire scene (from left to right).

Jefferson Ice fire, 1978, on Edison Court.

Fire ground operations on the SE corner of Clayton and N. Sheridan Road (photo taken from the News Sun Building).

Station 4 personnel (C Shift) Lt. Andy Twombly, Fire Fighters Brian Jacobi, Dan Brown, Rick Van Horn and Brian Rau.

C Shift personnel pose for photo after fighting a fire at 914 Glen Flora, (left to right) Fire Fighters Sean Barbosa, Scott Repec, Marco Vazquez, Steve Mudrak, Brad Buntrock, and Lt. Kevin Gartley.

Right: Fire personnel at Station 2: (C Shift, left to right) Fire Fighters Laura lea Thomas, Barry Loyal, and Lt. Jeffrey Welch.

Bottom: Waukegan fire fighters extinguishing fire at The Shoot O Rama on Greenwood Avenue at the Lake Front.

Station 2, dedicated in 1997.

Fire at the Karcher Hotel on Washington Street where 9 perished in 1984, Christmas Eve.

Fire personnel at Station 5: (A Shift, left to right) Fire Fighter Tom McCarthy, Lt. Tom Zelenz, and Fire Fighter Ron Grant.

Fire personnel at Station 2: (B Shift, left to right) Lt. Tim Needham, Fire Fighters Lauralea Thomas, and Jeremy Brown.

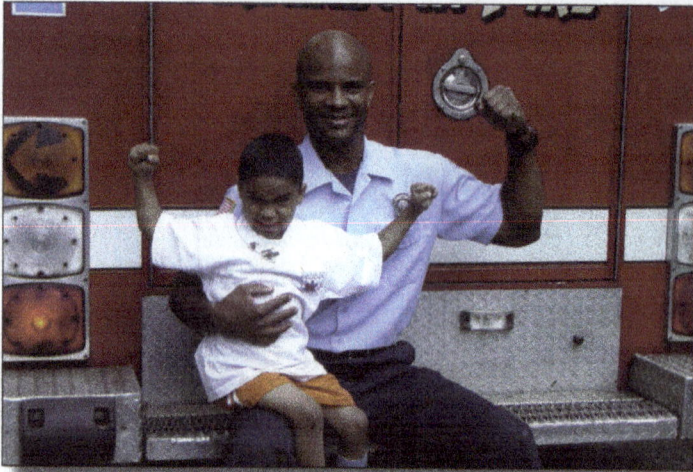

Fire Fighter George Bridges with a child that he aided by treating his life threatening injuries.

Fire Fighters Tom Richards and Steve Orusa at training fire.

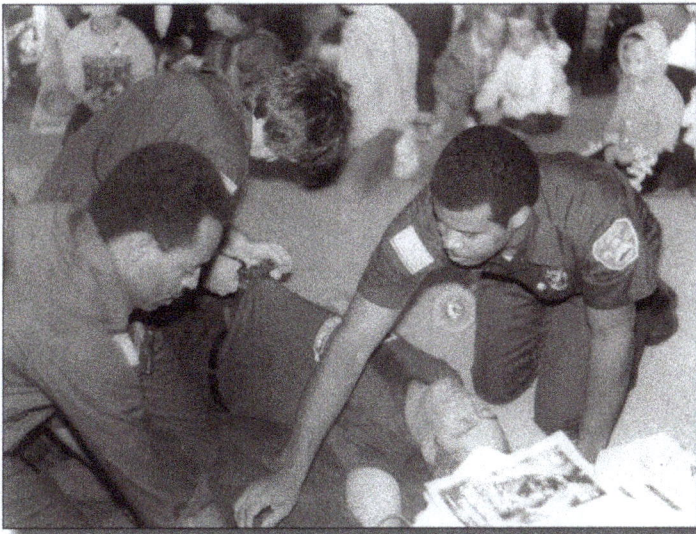

Fire Department Paramedics (left to right) Darnell Wright, Patrick Gallagher, and Ricco Farrell demonstrated a cardiac arrest call while Lt. Jim McGrain acts the part of a heart attack victim.

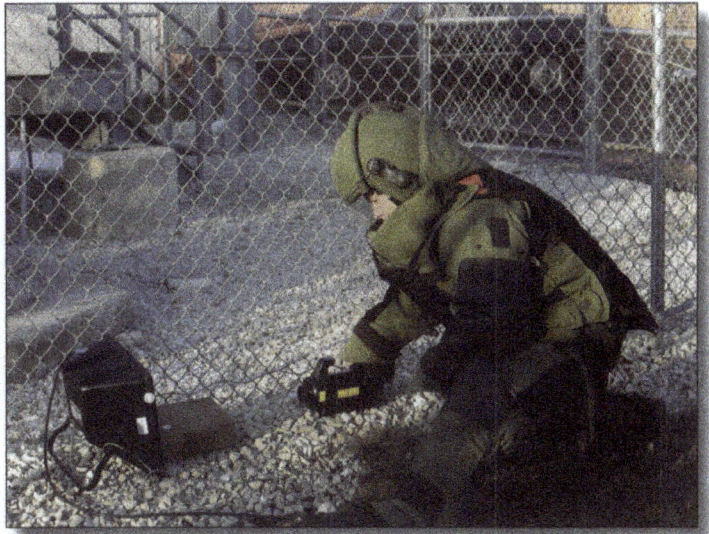

Lt. Tom Christensen demonstrates the use of the Hazardous Device Suit.

People's Choice Video Store fire on Grand Avenue, April 27, 1997.

Photo of fire fighter and equipment at the Tannery fire.

Fire personnel at Station 3, (B Shift, left to right) Fire Fighter Marco Vazquez, Tony Soler, Lt. Mark DeRose, Fire Fighter Mark Pietraszak, and Al Ramos.

Lt. Steve Fedor demonstrates the lifting of the 175 pound dead weight during participation of the fire department physical skills tessting.

Personnel at Station 3, (left to right) Fire Fighter Ted Casper, Brian Marks, Lt. Joel Verbrick, Fire Fighter Dan Romano, and Matthew Burleson.

Initial hiring photo of the following fire fighters 5-14-1987. From left to right: John Skillman, Dave Erdal, Tom Christensen, Robert Heraver, Melvin Pettis, and Ed Lindenmulder.

Bottom: Waukegan Fire Department's 1921 Stutz in all its glory traveling down Genesee Street.

Academy Theatre Fire Truck Operations.

Fire Fighters (left to right) are Daniel Crane, Dan Simmet, Lt. Ron Colpeart, Martin Davault and Steve Harling.

Firefighters (left to right) Jack Kruse Jr., Jon Nordgren, Lt. Mark (Grumpy) DeRose, Mark Pietraszak, Adam Slade.

Waukegan Oshkosh ARFF Unit at Station 5 for Aircraft fire fighting operations.

Captain George Opitz (Truck Door) examines new ladder truck with (left to right) Lt. James Hushour, Commissioner Edward Pavelick, and First Ward Alderman look on, April 19, 1977.

Capt. Mike Hutchison, Fire Fighters Jack Long and Marco Vazquez pose (left to right) in front of Truck 3.

Fire Fighters (left to right) Chris Ferguson, George Bridges, Ken Mayfield and Steve Mudrak pose in front of Squad 1.

Battalion Chief Ricco Farrell

Capt. Dan Wright (right) raises flag during 9-11 Ceremony at the Lake County Building.

Index

Fire Station and equipment at the turn of the 20th century.

www.ingramcontent.com/pod-product-compliance
Lightning Source LLC
Chambersburg PA
CBHW081414160426

42812CB00086B/1907